NAMES OF
GOD'S
PROMISES

NAMES OF GOD'S PROMISES

MARK A. TABB

MOODY PRESS
CHICAGO

© 1998 by
MARK A. TABB

ISBN: 0-8024-6183-2

1 3 5 7 9 10 8 6 4 2

Printed in the United States of America

To Bethany, Hannah, and Sarah.
May you learn to rely always upon God's promises.

His divine power has given us everything we need for life and godliness through our knowledge of him who called us by his own glory and goodness. Through these he has given us his very great and precious promises. (2 Peter 1:3–4a)

CONTENTS

Part 3:
Promises that Set Believers'
Lives Apart from the World

Part 4:
Promises that Carry Us
Through the Harshness of Life

INTRODUCTION:
THE WAKE-UP CALL

I'm going along in the flow of life, enjoying the ride. My daughters are healthy, my marriage is strong, my job secure. Minor troubles occasionally arise, but they hit everyone. No major tragedies have come my way for a very long time. I read my Bible, I pray, and I go to church. I try to put my faith into action as best I can. There are struggles, but nothing I cannot deal with. God has been good to me. Life is sweet.

Perhaps too sweet.

Without realizing it, I find I am operating on autopilot in my walk with God. I've become so accustomed to His blessings that I rarely stop and ponder the wonder of all that He has done for me. Call it ingratitude. Call it negligence. God calls it sin.

I don't know how it happens. Standing on top of the mountain of God's promises, I rarely give a thought to that which makes life worth living, to that which makes this existence life. Don't get me wrong. I think about God. I call out to Him. I try to follow Him by faith. But I find it is all too easy to forget that without His faithfulness to His Word I am nothing. And so are you.

The pages that follow take us on a journey through the mountaintops of Scripture. Through them we will explore the names of God's promises. The following promises assure us that Someone is thinking about us. They remind us that God loves and cares for us. Indeed, He loves to open the windows of heaven and pour out His very best on you and me. Yet the promises that follow are not about us. We need to remember that little detail. It is easy to forget.

There are times as I contemplate all that God has promised to do for me that my mind runs to the mistaken conclusion that I am the center of this party. I start to act as though God does all that He does for me and you because He has to. Consider the evidence: He wants us to be happy; He wants us to experience love and joy and peace; He wants to bless our lives. It sounds crazy, I know, but deep down in the inner recesses of my mind the thought comes to me that the mighty Lord of the universe exists for my good pleasure.

But the Bible tells us that *we exist for Him*. He does not exist for us. Everything He does, He does in such a way that His name will be magnified throughout all creation. Heaven's bands play for God alone. The choirs of angels sing His praise, not ours. As all of the invisible universe ponders the grace He has shown to the human race, it erupts in praise for Him. Not us.

I know this is sort of a somber introduction for a subject as uplifting as the promises of God. Believe me, my original intent was to start off on a high note and soar. But a funny thing happened as I began to list the names of the promises God makes in His Word. I found myself face-to-face with my utter dependence on the Lord. Apart from Him I really am nothing. Everything that I am, everything that I have, everything that I hope for, I owe it all to His kindness. All that makes life worth living flows forth from God and His promises. Even life itself, the continued existence of the universe, depends on Him. A humbling thought. Totally, completely, humbling.

As my mind pondered these things I immediately did the only logical thing a human being can do in such a situation: I dropped my head and began to praise God. And then it hit me. I suddenly realized that most Christians rarely stop and think about the promises of God. Instead, we walk through life oblivious to our dependence on them. When disaster strikes or the doctor breaks bad news to us or our job is downsized out of existence, then we run to the concordance and search for a word of encouragement. God's promises become our lifeline, lifting us to safety. We cry out for His mercy, His grace, His deliverance, His faithfulness to His Word.

After a while life goes back to normal and the promises that pulled us through are pushed back out of sight, out of mind.

Maybe I'm the only guilty party. Maybe I'm the only one who could be so thoughtless, so ungrateful. But I don't think so. The pages that follow are meant to be a wake-up call to all of us. Yes, we will explore the promises that bring us comfort and hope in times of trouble. But I long for these pages to do more than stimulate your mind or stir your emotions. I pray that they will focus our attention on the incomprehensible grace of our Lord. These

names of promises that roll off our tongues with the
greatest of ease—names like *salvation, life, peace,
joy, hope, protection, comfort,* and *love*—make life
worth living.

Come with me. Let's explore these names together. Many of the concepts are like old friends,
truths we have grown up with and grown accustomed to. It is time for us to become reacquainted.
It is time for us to rediscover their wonder as
though we were viewing them for the very first
time. It is time for us to remember how much we
owe to the love of God.

The first group of promises we will explore
flow out of the gift of God's Son. The second group
are promises God makes to us about His character
and actions toward us. The third set of promises set
our lives apart from the rest of the world. Finally,
we will spend some time with the promises that
help us face the harshness of reality. In the midst we
will find God reassuring us that He can use anything and everything for His purpose and glory.

We will begin our journey with the one promise
upon which all others rest, the promise that God
offers to every human creature on the planet, a
promise very few ever accept.

Part 1

PROMISES THAT
FLOW FROM
GOD'S GIFT OF HIS SON

1

THE NAME OF PROMISE

> An angel of the Lord . . . said, "Joseph son
> of David, do not be afraid to take Mary home
> as your wife, because what is conceived in
> her is from the Holy Spirit. She will give
> birth to a son, and you are to give him the
> name Jesus, because he will save his people
> from their sins." *(Matthew 1:20–21)*

The Bible is more than a book. It is God's Word, His message to all mankind. The words of Scripture communicate theological truth. They tell us who God is and what He is like. But the Bible does not stop there. God's message to the crowning point of His creation is a message of promise. Beginning with God's first recorded conversation with human beings, to His parting words at the close of the book of Revelation the theme of promise intertwines every story, every prophecy, every line of poetry, every word.

This does not mean that every line of Scripture contains a distinctive promise that we can write down and claim as our own. No, it means much more. The message of promise is the beginning and end of everything that is included in the Bible. It undergirds every word, sometimes openly, sometimes subtly, but it is always there. God's promises are the common thread that unites the Old and New Testaments, the core that makes sixty-six books into one.

All of the promises of God can be summarized in just one word, one name—the name that is

above every name. Every promise is somehow con-
nected to this name, for the One who bears it came
both to fulfill them all and to offer them to all of
mankind. Without Him none of the other promises
means anything. To reject Him is to reject every
promise in the Book. But to those who receive Him,
He gives the unique privilege of becoming a child
of God, a child of promise.

The One who embodies all of the promises of God
bears many names. Scripture calls Him Immanuel, the
Word, Son of Man, Son of God, Lion of Judah, Bread of
Life, and many more. We know Him best by one
name. The name of promise. The name Jesus.

When God instructed Mary and Joseph through
His angel to name their Son Jesus, He gave a name
not at all unique or uncommon. Many Jewish boys
in the first century were named Jesus, or, more fa-
miliar to us, Joshua. It was a name of honor, a name
enriched by the man who led the children of Israel's
conquest of Canaan. The name is a form of the Hebrew word that means salvation. When the Lord
placed this name upon His Son, He proclaimed to
all the world that the Savior had arrived. The child
born in a barn in Bethlehem was and is the one
hope of all mankind. This Joshua—Jesus—was the
One who would "save His people from their sins."

This was Jesus' mission. Listen to the way Jesus
Himself described it in the third chapter of the book
of John: "For God so loved the world that he gave his
one and only Son, that whoever believes in him shall
not perish but have eternal life. For God did not send
his Son into the world to condemn the world, but to
save the world through him" (verses 16–17).

Jesus came to save the world.

As the average American's level of biblical knowledge drops to lower and lower levels, we forget what this means. Without Jesus, the citizens of planet Earth exist in a hopeless state of separation from God. A terminal condition called *sin* infects all of us. Sin is more than an occasional slip of profanity or little white lies. It is a way of life where we refuse to submit to the Lord's rule over our lives and assert our own authority. All of us are infected. We may try to deny it or to hide it, but sin has this unfortunate habit of bubbling to the surface through acts we would rather not admit to. The fact that we like sin makes our condition even more hopeless.

Before long our sin catches up with us through death. Our lives go on for a short span of time and then they end. All that we accomplished is forgotten, our memory fades with the passing of time. We go to the grave empty-handed. But death is not the end. It is a permanent condition where creatures designed for fellowship with God are eternally separated from Him. To make matters worse, there is absolutely nothing any of us can do to change this fate. We cannot save ourselves.

What we could not do, God did by sending His Son. Jesus, the eternal Word, took on human flesh and became one of us. Every day He found Himself bombarded by temptation, but He never gave in. But simply coming to earth in human flesh and refraining from sin wasn't enough to save mankind from the fate that hangs over our heads. He had to do something about the sentence of death. And He did, by dying in our place. Three days later He walked out of the tomb, having defeated sin and death.

Now God makes this promise to everyone who

is willing to listen. Anyone, regardless of the color
of their skin, regardless of their national origin, regardless of their social class and standing,
regardless of anything they have ever done in the
past, anyone who believes in Jesus Christ will be
saved (Acts 16:31). The Lord promises to take all of
our sin and cancel it. Through Jesus He vows to
plant a new heart within us, a heart that longs to
know God and to please Him (Jeremiah 31:33–34).

All that follows in the pages of this book rests
upon this promise. Only those who accept God's
offer of salvation through Christ can lay claim to
the promises found in His Word. God isn't narrow-
minded. He doesn't play favorites. But the only
place His promises can be found is in His Son.
Those who search for them in some other place will
discover nothing but disappointment. Everyone
who comes humbly to Christ will find in Him everything they could possibly desire.

If you have never received God's gift of salvation that He promises in His Son, you can right
now by faith. Romans 10:9 makes this promise to
you, "If you confess with your mouth, 'Jesus is
Lord,' and believe in your heart that God raised
him from the dead, you will be saved." To make
this promise your own you simply need to call on
the name of the Lord in prayer "for everyone who
calls on the name of the Lord will be saved" (Romans 10:13). Tell Him you are tired of going your
own direction, you are sick of your sin. Ask Him to
forgive you and He will. Invite Him to come into
your life and take control of it. His promise is real.
Anyone who calls on the name of the Lord will be
saved. Even you, even now. God guarantees it.

2

LIFE

"The thief comes only to steal and kill and destroy; I have come that they may have life, and have it to the full." *(John 10:10)*

It doesn't feel much like living—"getting by," that's a more accurate description. Or surviving. Or existing. It is not what we expected. We have everything we need: food, clothing, shelter, transportation, all the essentials of life. But somehow the essentials seem inadequate. They are not working. We crave something more.

Voices shout at us from every direction, trying to tell us what that something more may be. Advertisers bombard us with everything from weight-loss plans to decadently delicious chocolate, all promising to add a little zing to life. And life does look exciting in those thirty-second splashes. Maybe we should ignore the product and copy the lifestyles of those daring young men and women with their carbonated beverages. Thrills and chills may be the something more we are looking for. A little bungee jumping or skydiving or at the very least, a ride on one of Kings Island's latest roller coasters, would shake the cobwebs out of the mind and get life on track. Maybe we just need to have a little more fun or more stuff or more calories or more caffeine;

maybe that is all we need for existence to feel like life.

Or maybe we are confused.

We long for life but settle for existence. Deep down inside we think we know what we are looking for. *Life should be an adventure, or at least an enjoyable experience,* we tell ourselves. But it is not. We long for life, but settle for the daily grind. We long for adventure but settle for punching a clock at a job we despise. We long for romance but settle for living alongside someone who shares our last name. We long for so much but settle for so little.

In the midst of this tension between the life we long for and the existence we endure, we hear Jesus say, "I have come that [you] may have life, and have it to the full" (John 10:10).

Jesus' words sound like the very thing we are looking for, if we only understood what He was talking about. We know He promises to give us a life so full that an eternity is required to squeeze in everything He has planned for us. Most of us assume this eternal life will be noticeably different than anything we experienced before. It should have more joy and less heartache, more purpose and less emptiness, more pizzazz and less ho-hum. If God plans it, then surely it will be interesting.

John 10:10 isn't the only place God promises to give us life to the full. From Genesis to Revelation this promise turns up in the Bible time after time after time. God promised Abraham the joy of fatherhood, yet he spent twenty-five years waiting for a son. God promised Moses the adventure of being the long-awaited deliverer of the children of Israel, an adventure that turned into forty years of wandering around in the Sinai wilderness dragging a reluctant people toward the Promised Land. God promised Jeremiah the privilege of being His voice to the kings and leaders of Judah, yet no one ever listened to even one of his sermons. God repeated His promise of abundant life through His Son—the Son who later died upon the cross.

Funny thing, every time God promises to give us life He forgets to mention thrills and excitement. Listen to Jesus' own definition of the life He came to give us: "Now this is eternal life: that they may know you, the only true God, and Jesus Christ, whom you have sent" (John 17:3). Notice, Jesus didn't say life comes through knowing about God. Rather, eternal life means knowing God in an intimate, personal relationship.

Maybe this is why so few ever find the life they are looking for. It is found in a place where few of us ever think to look. God has always defined life in this way. The first man and woman were created to know God. They died spiritually when they were driven out of His presence, even though their bodies continued to function. Our search for life takes us many places and causes us to sample many things, but the hunger that keeps us from ever being satisfied with anything is the hunger for God Himself.

Once we come to know Him—once we find the promise of life—our lives will be markedly different. Listen to Paul's words in his letter to the church in Colossae:

> *Since, then, you have been raised with Christ, set your hearts on things above, where Christ is seated at the*

right hand of God. . . . For you died, and your life is now hidden with Christ in God. . . . Put to death, therefore, whatever belongs to your earthly nature. (Colossians 3:1, 3, 5)

Something is missing from life. Nothing this world has to offer can satisfy the longing that God has planted deep inside us. But once we discover the joy of God's promise of life, we will begin throwing off those things that characterized our lives before. Their appeal will be gone. Life in Christ sets our hearts and minds on the things above, the things of God, the things that are real and enduring.

Here is the promise of life that goes beyond existence, life that fulfills the purpose God had for you and me when He breathed into the nostrils of the first man. Life that is worth living means knowing God. Until we come to know Him, all we are doing is marking time on planet Earth. We have not yet begun to live.

3

FORGIVENESS

If we confess our sins, he is faithful and
just and will forgive us our sins and purify
us from all unrighteousness. *(1 John 1:9)*

Let's pretend for a moment that you are in debt.
For most of us, we don't have to stretch our
imaginations too far to know what being in debt
feels like; every month our car, mortgage, and credit card payments remind us. But suppose you owe
an amount so enormous the minimum monthly
payment exceeds your *annual* income. This debt is
so huge that your calculator does not have enough
spaces for all the zeroes, and you are solely responsible for repayment. What would you do?

I do not know how one person could accumu-
late a debt of this magnitude, but Jesus told a story
of someone who had:

> The kingdom of heaven is like a king who wanted to set-
> tle accounts with his servants. As he began the settlement,
> a man who owed him ten thousand talents was brought
> to him. Since he was not able to pay, the master ordered
> that he and his wife and his children and all that he had
> be sold to repay the debt. (Matthew 18:23–25)

The poor soul in Jesus' story owed ten thousand talents, a strange amount to Western ears. To
fully appreciate his situation, we need to know that

a talent was the highest known denomination of currency in the ancient Roman Empire. A single talent was equal to three thousand denarii, or the amount that it would take the average worker three thousand days, or nearly ten years, to earn. This servant owed not one but *ten thousand* talents. If he gave every penny he made to the king, it would take him nearly one hundred *thousand* years to repay his debt. Without a doubt, he owed a debt he could not pay.

Jesus' point in telling this story was not to educate us about the finer points of ancient Near Eastern finance. The king in the story is the King of Kings, God Himself. And the servant in the story is not some deadbeat far away in a distant land. He represents you and me. We don't have to pretend that we owe an amount equal to the national debt. Someday when we stand before God we will discover that we owe Him an amount far greater.

I don't know how the man in Jesus' story accumulated his debt, but I know how we put ourselves in this predicament. We took something much greater than money from the Lord. We tried to steal His kingdom away from Him. Every time we choose to reject His authority over our lives, we still carry out a coup against His throne. Every time we willfully do that which we know displeases Him, we fire shots of rebellion in His direction. Every time we do the right thing for the wrong reason or claim that our lives are fine without His influence, we assert that we, not God, are sovereign over our universe. You cannot put a price tag on the debt our actions have accumulated.

When the servant in Jesus' story was brought

before the king and was commanded to pay up or
be sold into slavery, he fell on his knees and pleaded for mercy. Anyone in his position would do the
same thing. With a debt so large, the only hope is
grace. We expect to see the servant pleading before
the king, but we do not expect the Master's response. He took pity on the servant, canceled the
debt, and let him go (Matthew 18:27). I do not understand how or why the king in the story would
cancel a debt so large without demanding some
sort of justice. Reading the story, we tend to focus
on the good fortune of the man who received mercy, while it is easy to forget the cost of forgiveness to
the king. With the stroke of a pen the king gave up
his claim to a fortune and his right to punish the
man who squandered away so much money.

Long ago, when I was a child, my mother
taught me to say my prayers before I went to bed.
One line was always a part of those simple prayers,
". . . and forgive anything I have done that displeases you." As I grew up, so did my prayer until it
reached a climax when I asked Christ to be my
Lord and Savior. But that wasn't the end of my need
for the simple prayer my mother taught me to pray.
First John 1:9 reminds us that God's promise of forgiveness stretches across the lifetime of a believer.
There God assures us that "if we will confess our
sins, he is faithful and just and will forgive us our
sins and purify us from all unrighteousness." I find
that as I pray for forgiveness for specific acts that
displease God, He has already granted my request
even before I ask.

In this cycle of asking and receiving forgiveness, it is all too easy to forget what forgiveness cost

God. The words roll from my lips with the greatest of ease, but the gift I seek came at the price of Jesus' life. Unlike the king in the parable, God did not pay a financial expense. Ten thousand talents, as valuable as it is, pales in comparison to the death of the Son of God. The penalty for sin is death. We owe it, we deserve it. God could not simply overlook our acts. To do so would compromise His holiness and His character. Therefore, He carried out an act of love so great that our minds cannot understand it. He sacrificed His Son so that you and I can be forgiven.

Jesus adds one more detail to the story of the debtor in the parable. After the man received mercy from the king, he went out and found a man who owed him a hundred denarii, a paltry sum in comparison to his own debt. When he found him, the man who had received mercy grabbed the one who owed him a few hundred dollars and began to choke him, demanding repayment. We gasp, wondering how anyone could be so heartless in light of the great mercy he himself had received. But we rarely think twice about holding a grudge against someone who cuts us off in traffic or cheats us out of a few dollars. We stomp and scream and demand justice, all the while enjoying the fruits of God's mercy.

The promise of forgiveness must move us to the act of forgiveness. As God has forgiven us, we are to forgive others. Until we do we still do not understand the promise. Nor have we received it.

4

MERCY

As a father has compassion on his children,
so the Lord has compassion on those who
fear him; for he knows how we are formed, he
remembers that we are dust. *(Psalm 103:13–14)*

The moments are all too rare. Most of us will experience only a handful during our lifetimes. These are those rare occasions when it feels as though the Lord sweeps away the barriers between heaven and earth, takes us in His arms, and speaks to us. He doesn't use an audible voice. Instead He focuses our attention upon a particular passage of Scripture and whispers, "I made sure these words were in the Book for you. I knew that you would need to hear this right now. I wrote it just for you." From that moment forward we can never again look at that particular passage in the same way. No longer is it the musings of someone long since dead. When the Lord speaks through His Word, it comes alive, a dynamic life-changing force.

This experience is the heart of one of God's most precious promises to us, the promise of mercy. God's mercy is far more than a decree by which He cancels out the consequences of our sin. The promise describes the way He deals with you and me on a daily basis. Listen to the words of Jeremiah the prophet in Lamentations 3:

I remember my affliction and my wandering,
      the bitterness and the gall.
I well remember them,
      and my soul is downcast within me.
Yet this I call to mind
      and therefore I have hope:
Because of the Lord's great love we are not consumed,
      for his compassions never fail.
They are new every morning;
      great is your faithfulness. (verses 19–23)

I grew up singing a hymn based on these words. I never thought much about what the hymn actually said. I was far too busy making sure I hit the right notes or thinking about the Dallas Cowboys football game that would kick off as soon as church ended. But late one night all of that changed. Not only did that night open my eyes to Jeremiah's message, it allowed me to understand the absolute joy and wonder of God's mercy.

On that night God spoke through the words you just read. I could relate to Jeremiah's complaint. My life felt like one great big dose of affliction and gall. All I wanted to do was go to bed and not get up for a month. I was more than depressed; I was worn out. A series of trials had taken their toll and I could not take another step. And then God intervened. I do not know how I ended up in the book of Lamentations. For that matter, I do not know why I opened my Bible at one o'clock in the morning. But when I did, the Lord riveted my eyes to these words and then whispered to me, "This is for you." Nothing changed in the trials I faced and yet everything changed.

Lamentations 3:22–23 makes to us the promise

of compassion and mercy. (The Hebrew word translated *compassions* is elsewhere translated *mercies*.) That promise took on flesh when God sent His Son to earth. Compassion marked Jesus' every movement. From His tenderness shown the woman at the well to His mercy shown the thief on the cross, Jesus demonstrated the true character of God. This same compassion is available to us when we plunge our lives upon Christ; in mercy He will save and lead us. Jesus is the one who sympathizes with our weaknesses so that "we may receive mercy and find grace to help us in our time of need" (Hebrews 4:16).

Mercy assures us that God is aware of everything we are going through. It reminds us that He will make sure the storms of life do not blow us away. His compassion will shelter us and carry us through; "they are new every morning." Our Lord knows what our mornings can be like. He knows all about those days when we wake up and feel like pulling the covers over our heads or throwing the alarm clock out the window, when the last thing we want to do is face a group of children with one thing on their mind: "What's for breakfast?" Our Lord knows about those mornings when the thought of going to work causes a burning pain to churn in our stomach. When we lie in bed wondering how we can face another day, God finds a new way to shower His compassion upon us.

Sometimes we have a completely different idea about the character of God. Far too often we see Him as a stern, hard-to-please disciplinarian. We want to please Him, desperately. We frequently find it hard to look at ourselves in the mirror when our lives do not live up to the example Christ set for us when He walked on the earth. Far too often we become so focused on what it takes to please God that we forget that He is already pleased with us because of the Cross of Christ.

This conception of God results in legalism and something much worse. It prevents children of God from drawing close to their Father, who loves them with a love their minds cannot comprehend. The psalmist gives us a fresh new perspective on our failings and God's expectations in Psalm 103:13–14. Notice the Lord's compassion is like that of a father who shows compassion to his children: "As a father has compassion on his children, so the Lord has compassion on those who fear him; for he knows how we are formed, he remembers that we are dust."

"As a father has compassion"; I love that line. And "He knows how we are formed, he remembers that we are dust." God is not surprised by our shortcomings. He isn't shocked when we fail to measure up to His standards. Yet He loves us anyway. Why? Because of His great mercy.

None of this means we should sin so that God's grace might increase. Far from it. Because God loves us, we want to show our love for Him by pleasing Him in everything we do. But remember, our Lord's hands don't hold a wooden spoon with which to smack us when we fail. Instead, His hands are scarred by the ends He was willing to go through to make us His children. Those same hands will someday wipe away every tear from our eyes. His mercy truly will be shown throughout all eternity.

5

SECURITY

"Be strong and courageous . . . for the
Lord your God goes with you; he will never
leave you nor forsake you." *(Deuteronomy
31:6)*

It's out there. Hiding, waiting, watching. A master of
disguise, it constantly changes its appearance and
attacks us when we least expect it. Its aliases make
up a who's who of our nightmares, things like . . .

Monsters under the bed. Sharks. Spiders.

The dark. Speaking in public. Heights.

Death.

Failure.

Financial ruin.

Rejection.

None of us is immune. We all feel its icy grip—
the grip of fear. Just in case any of us breaks free, a
group of scientists and other government employ-
ees work round the clock coming up with new
things for us to be afraid of. They fill the six o'clock
news with stories of nuclear terrorism, global
warming, multinational economic meltdown, and
even alien invasions! Just thinking about it makes
me want to run down to the hardware store to buy
another deadbolt for the front door.

In the midst of so much fear, so much uncer-
tainty, the Bible assures us that we never have to
worry about God turning His back on us. Nothing

in all the world is big enough or strong enough to separate us from His love. The apostle Paul put it this way:

> *Who shall separate us from the love of Christ? Shall trouble or hardship or persecution or famine or nakedness or danger or sword? For I am convinced that neither death nor life, neither angels nor demons, neither the present nor the future, nor any powers, neither height nor depth, nor anything else in all creation, will be able to separate us from the love of God that is in Christ Jesus our Lord. (Romans 8:35, 38–39)*

In an uncertain world, during this age of angst, a time when paranoia and conspiracy theories abound, we have nothing to fear, for we are secure in Christ Jesus.

Long before Paul penned these words, Isaiah the prophet compared God's love for us to the love a mother has for her newborn child. The prophet asked this rhetorical question, "Can a mother forget the baby at her breast and have no compassion on the child she has borne?" (Isaiah 49:15). As anyone who has ever spent any time around a new mother can tell you, the answer is a resounding "No." Mothers have this instinctive ability to hear the faintest noise a newborn makes. They lock onto the sound of their child's voice like radar and immediately spring into action the second the child utters the slightest cry.

There is more to this promise the Lord voiced through Isaiah: "Though she may forget, I will not forget you! See, I have engraved you on the palms of my hands" (verses 15–16). Our Lord cannot forget you or me when we belong to Him. He has a

constant reminder of His love for us before Him engraved on the palms of His hands. A mark made
with ink could be washed off or would wear away
with time. Therefore the Lord is pictured as cutting
a reminder of His children into His hands that will
last forever.

I doubt that Isaiah fully appreciated the im-
agery of the words flowing from his pen. I cannot
read his words without thinking about the reminder of God's love that is cut into the hands of
His Son, the marks made by the nails of the cross.
Those scars aren't the only reminder of His love for
us, a love that stretches back long before the beginning of time. Ephesians 1:4 assures us that He
chose us before the creation of the world. In the
fullness of time He sent His Son to die on our behalf. By His sovereign power He orchestrated the
events of our lives to bring us to the place where we
said yes to His offer of eternal life. Even the faith by
which we cling to Christ comes to us as a gift from
God.

No wonder nothing can separate us from His
love. How could He stop loving someone for whom
He died? How could He suddenly forget someone
whose life He has foreseen since before the founda-
tions of the earth were laid? How could He turn His
back on someone He is transforming in the image
of His Son?

Just as nothing can separate us from His love,
nothing can separate us from His presence. When
we accept Christ as our personal Savior, the Holy
Spirit of God takes up residence inside of us. By doing so He fulfills the promise Jesus made to His
disciples shortly before He ascended into heaven, "I

will be with you always, to the very end of the age"
(Matthew 28:20). His children will never experience one second disconnected from Him. Even in
those moments when we do not want Him around,
those times when we choose to do that which displeases Him, He is there. The pangs of conviction
and guilt are evidence that He loves us too much to
abandon us to sin or anything else.

The Lord makes this promise to us: "'Never
will I leave you; never will I forsake you.' So we can
say with confidence, 'The Lord is my helper; I will
not be afraid. What can man do to me?'" (Hebrews
13:5–6).

And that is the point. Because we are secure in
Christ we have nothing to fear, not even big creepy
spiders.

6

VICTORY

Everyone born of God overcomes the world. This is the victory that has overcome the world, even our faith. Who is it that overcomes the world? Only he who believes that Jesus is the Son of God. (1 John 5:4–5)

Dig a little deeper. Make those walls a little wider. Fill the storerooms; it could be a long wait. Grab the kids and stay here where it is safe, inside the bunker. Outside a war rages. Bad people intend to do Christians harm. Stories have already begun to trickle in from the front lines, stories of people like us being misunderstood, mistreated, misled, and just plain missing. Only a fool would venture out into the cross fire. Hide in here with us, inside the bunker.

Inside the bunker, we have a safe, sanitized, Christianized culture. We have schools and books and music and television shows, and even our own exercise classes, long-distance phone companies, T-shirts, and radio stations. You don't have to worry about bad people sneaking up and leading you astray. Here in the bunker most of us look alike, talk alike, and think alike, even though we seldom believe alike on every point. If we disagree too much, we simply build another bunker. We don't have to get along; we just want to survive.

Without the bunker, we may not. Some of our ancient ancestors tried to live without one, and

they became destitute, persecuted, and mistreated.
Some were tortured, others faced jeers and flog-
gings, while still others were chained and put in
prison. The same thing could happen today. It's a
jungle out there, you know. Those people in the
world, they don't like us. The movies and television
shows make fun of us; their music offends us.
While we've never actually been persecuted, being
misunderstood by the next-door neighbor is no
bed of roses.

I think I'll boycott the world and hide here in
my Christian bunker until Jesus comes back.

Ridiculous? Of course. Unfortunately a siege
mentality has settled upon many of us who claim to
follow Jesus Christ. We hear talk of culture wars
and the erosion of First Amendment rights and we
become afraid. The nightly news brings to our
doorstep reminders of the loss of morality, and we
don't know what to do about it. Church attendance
is stagnant, the influence of Christianity upon our
culture is evaporating, and the prophets in the pul-
pits tell us things are only going to get worse. In
response we try to insulate ourselves and our children from the world. We hunker down against
defeat as the spiritual battles rage around us.

Yet defeat is exactly the opposite of what our
Lord promised us in the fifth chapter of First John:
"Everyone born of God overcomes the world. This
is the victory that has overcome the world, even
our faith. Who is it that overcomes the world? Only
he who believes that Jesus is the Son of God" (verses
4–5). Jesus promised us victory.

Jesus never hid from the world. Paul never
shrank back from the arena of the exchange of ideas.

John ended up in exile on the rocky island of Patmos because he refused to remain silent. Elijah and Elisha, Jeremiah and Amos all stayed on the offensive for the Lord, never retreating. They all walked in victory, even when it cost them their lives.

God's promise of victory is not reserved for the distant future at the end of time. It is more than the ultimate "I told you so" to a hostile world. Victory is a way of life for those who follow the Son of God. Everyone who is born of God overcomes the world. Every day, in every way, victory follows those who follow the Son.

This doesn't mean that our culture will suddenly become Christianized or that gangsta rap music will be banned. If history teaches us anything, it tells us that the light of the gospel always shines brightest when the world is the darkest. The victory that our Lord allows us to experience means we can overcome the world even if the world refuses to be changed.

Pastor Samuel Lamb knows what it means to live in victory. Twenty-one of his seventy-two years have been spent in prison courtesy of the communist government of China. As recently as 1990 the house church he serves as pastor was closed by government officials and all of his property confiscated. But Pastor Lamb didn't shrink back. He continued doing what God called him to do. As Cal Thomas reported in his syndicated column (July 6, 1997), Lamb's church, without a building, averaged four hundred worshipers in 1997 during each of its four services a week. The Public Security Bureau continues to keep an eye on him, but it stopped persecuting him with the old ferocity.

As Pastor Lamb put it, "Each time they arrested me and sent me off to prison, the church grew. Persecution was good for us. The more they persecuted, the more the church grew. That's been the history of the church."

It is also God's promise. Pastor Lamb and innumerable other believers in communist China embody the promise we find in the book of Revelation, "They overcame him by the blood of the Lamb and by the word of their testimony; they did not love their lives so much as to shrink from death" (Revelation 12:11).

We will overcome, for it is impossible for us to lose. Impossible! The war is already over. Jesus won it early one Sunday morning when He walked out of the tomb alive. Now our living Lord calls us to leave our bunkers, go out into the world, and proclaim His victory for everyone to hear. Yes, we will face opposition. More people will tune us out than will listen. Some may be so offended that they try to silence us; yet they will not succeed, for everyone born of God, everyone who believes that Jesus is the Christ, overcomes the world. Those who doubt, hide . . . needlessly.

7

JUSTIFICATION

> There is no difference, for all have sinned and fall short of the glory of God, and are justified freely by his grace through the redemption that came by Christ Jesus. (*Romans 3:22–24*)

I was three or four, my sister six. I don't remember much about that afternoon thirty-something years ago. My sister remembers. Who could forget getting hit in the head with a brick by your little brother? Most of the details are sketchy in my mind, with one exception: I remember my airtight defense. My sister took my truck and wouldn't give it back. What choice did I have but to hit her over the head with the closest thing I could find? Was it my fault that a brick happened to be laying there? In one of the great miscarriages of justice this world has ever seen, the judge and jury, my mother, rejected my defense and punished me anyway.

I was framed, I tell you, an innocent victim of a corrupt system. My sister thinks I should still be grounded.

I didn't know it at the time, but I was engaging in one of the oldest activities the human race ever invented. We have an uncanny knack for justifying anything and everything we do. The trend started long before the invention of bricks or trucks, on the day sin entered the world. After Adam and Eve were caught disobeying God, they immediately be-

gan to make excuses. They proclaimed their own
innocence while pointing the finger of blame at the
snake slithering toward the bushes.

With the passing of time, we have refined
Adam and Eve's act of justifying into an art form.
We justify ourselves in many ways. Cheating on
taxes is never wrong, since tax rates are too high.
Stealing from the workplace is not a crime, since
the pitiful salaries they hand out are much too low.
Sexual infidelity can't be condemned, not when it
makes us happy. Divorce is downright virtuous
when we find ourselves trapped in an unhappy
marriage. Greed is just ambition, materialism stim-
ulates the economy, selfishness is thriftiness. And,
just in case we feel a small twinge of guilt, we can
comfort ourselves in the knowledge that "Everyone
else is doing it."

And they are. Everyone else is cheating and
stealing and lying and lusting. The Bible is exactly
right when it says, "There is no one righteous, not
even one; there is no one who understands, no one
who seeks God. All have turned away . . . there is
no one who does good, not even one" (Romans
3:10–12). Just in case any of us wanted to use ignorance as a defense, God clearly spells out what is
right and what is wrong in His Word. We love to
make excuses, to justify ourselves, but God's law
lets us know that He doesn't buy any of them. He
won't even listen to our most cherished line, "I'm
better than that guy over there." The entire world,
every human being on the face of the planet, stands
guilty and silent before God, without hope, without
excuses.

This dark, bleak picture sets the stage for the

wonder of the promise that seems too good to be
true. God in His infinite mercy and grace promises
to justify all those who have faith in Jesus:

> *For what the law was powerless to do in that it was*
> *weakened by the sinful nature, God did by sending his*
> *own Son in the likeness of sinful man to be a sin offering.*
> *And so he condemned sin in sinful man, in order that the*
> *righteous requirements of the law might be fully met in*
> *us, who do not live according to the sinful nature but ac-*
> *cording to the Spirit"* (Romans 8:3–4).

The difference between God's act of justifying
us and our justification of ourselves is this: God
does not affirm our present sinful condition. He
condemns our sin, yet He still finds a way to justify
the sinner. All of this is made possible through the
Cross.

By placing all of our sin upon His Son, God is
able to maintain His justice while also justifying
people like you and me (Romans 3:26). Through
Christ we can be free from blame and guilt. All of
the righteous requirements of the Law were met in
Jesus. By placing us in Christ, God meets those
same requirements in us. If this weren't amazing
enough, God takes His promise one step further
and offers it to anyone and everyone who will respond.

Sadly, most people are too busy justifying themselves to ever think that they need to be justified by
God. "Christ died for the ungodly" (Romans 5:6),
but we think that must surely be someone else. We
may be a little less than perfect, occasionally we tell
little white lies or use poor judgment, but ungodly?
That's taking things too far. And so the words of the

promise fall to the ground. They sound good, for the really desperate. But no one sees himself as desperate.

That is, until God goes to work. Few things are as humbling as the thought that I never would have accepted God's promise of justification if He had left me alone to make up my own mind. The promise would have been just as real, but I never would have responded. The only reason I said yes to Him was because His Holy Spirit persistently drew me to Himself. The same is true for you and for everyone else who finds this promise to be true. We owe everything to Him.

The promise of justification is more than a dry, theological concept. It should produce a sense of wonder and thanksgiving toward God, as well as tremendous freedom in day-to-day life. Real justification sets us free from the cycle of pitiful excuses and lame attempts to rebuild our image in the eyes of others. It allows us to admit our faults, confess our darkest sins, and walk with our heads held high, secure in the promise offered through the Cross.

8

ADOPTION

> We know that the whole creation has been groaning as in the pains of childbirth right up to the present time. Not only so, but we ourselves, who have the firstfruits of the Spirit, groan inwardly as we wait eagerly for our adoption as sons, the redemption of our bodies. For in this hope we were saved. (Romans 8:22–24)

The moments tick by and we sit, waiting. Sighs can he heard from around the room. Glancing at the clock doesn't do any good because we don't know when it is supposed to happen. And so we wait. And wait. And wait. A few experts in one corner of the room assure us that the hour is almost at hand. From time to time they will circle a specific day on the calendar as the day when our waiting will be over. But all of the circles are soon forgotten as their page of the calendar comes and goes just like every other calendar page. The waiting continues. The sighs in the room grow louder.

We don't wait for the day alone. Romans 8:22 tells us that all of creation anxiously awaits the day we will go home to join our Father. Paul compares creation's travail to the pains of childbirth (and we thought we alone were desperate to see the day arrive). Since the day sin entered the world the entire physical universe has been thrown into a state God never intended for it. If the ground and the plants and the animals could talk, if they could feel and express the full range of human emotion, we would hear a loud, overwhelming wail echoing across the earth. Creation is ready for the day when God's promise of adoption will reach its climax. "We know that the whole creation has been groaning. . . . Not only so, but we ourselves, who have the firstfruits of the Spirit, groan inwardly as we wait eagerly for our adoption as sons, the redemption of our bodies. For in this hope we were saved" (Romans 8:22–24).

God's promise of adoption falls within the tension between the "already" and "not yet" natures of His kingdom. The Bible tells us that the kingdom of God came to earth when Jesus arrived nearly two thousand years ago. He is the King of Kings and Lord of Lords who rules over the entire universe. But many parts of the universe, namely mankind, have not yet submitted themselves to His rule. Therefore we can say that the kingdom of God is already at hand while the full manifestation will arrive the day Christ returns.

The promise of adoption has the same dual characteristics. Everyone who receives Christ as his or her Savior through faith is received into the family of God through adoption at the moment of salvation. As Paul wrote in Ephesians 1:4–5, "In love he predestined us to be adopted as his sons." We don't have to prove ourselves worthy or work our way into God's favor. In love He adopts us so that we can truly say that we are sons and daughters of God.

It is not by chance that God directed His prophets to use the term *adoption* to describe how He made us a part of His family. Two thousand years ago and today, adopted children enjoy a unique protection by the law. They can never be disowned. In the ancient Near East, natural born children could be written out of a father's will, but the inheritance of an adopted child was guaranteed. In the same way, our position in Christ and the inheritance we long for are both guaranteed by God's promise.

This "already" aspect of adoption only heightens our anticipation for the "not yet" that lies ahead. Adoption is far more than a term describing a legal transaction or our new status with God. Paul equates our adoption as sons with the gift of the Holy Spirit, whom God pours out upon everyone who comes to Him by faith. Romans 8:15 describes the Holy Spirit as the Spirit of sonship, that is, adoption.

When God brings us into His family, He draws us into a close intimate relationship with Him. Through the Spirit we cry out to the Lord with words only a child could use, "*Abba,* Father." The term *Abba* is the Hebrew equivalent of our English term *Daddy.* When the Father adopts us into His family, all pretense and formality melts away. Like a child crying out for her daddy on a stormy night, we call out to Him and He hears us.

The promise of adoption assures us that our wait will not be long. God guarantees that someday soon He will send His Son to bring us home. On that day we will enter heaven with the same eager anticipation as children walking into their room at home for the very first time. Everything we could possibly desire will surround us, for the one thing we long for more than anything else is not a thing at all but a who—the Father Himself. The One who chose us, who adopted us into His family in spite of our imperfections, in spite of our constant failures, will be waiting at the door to take us up in His arms and hold us with an eternal embrace.

No wonder we groan inwardly as we await the completion of the adoption process. Our world can be a cold, cruel place. We long to feel the warmth of the Father's embrace. By faith we know He is near us now; but our eyes ache to actually see Him. The lives we live on planet Earth we live as adopted children of the King, but this place is not our home. We want to go home to be with our Father.

9

HEAVEN

> And I heard a loud voice from the throne saying, "Now the dwelling of God is with men, and he will live with them. They will be his people, and God himself will be with them and be their God. He will wipe every tear from their eyes. There will be no more death or mourning or crying or pain, for the old order of things has passed away." *(Revelation 21:3–4)*

I cannot wait for my first day—no, make that the first few seconds—in heaven. Oh, the joy, the unspeakable joy that moment will hold! I have no idea exactly how the transition is made from this world to the world to come. The Bible does not say anything about tunnels of light or any other such foolishness. It simply tells us that to be absent from the body is to be at home with the Lord. If I understand that promise correctly, then it appears that when we close our eyes for the last time in this life, we open them in the life to come.

Just think of it! One second we are looking out on a hospital room or a freeway or our own bedroom, the next we are in the midst of heaven's glory. The sound of millions of angels singing fills our ears, the light of the glory of God flashes before our eyes. We close our eyes quickly, rub them, open them again and strain to bring everything into focus. It cannot be a dream, for this experience is more real than anything we ever experienced on earth. Finally, at long last, we are home.

Home. Tears of joy surely must flow from our

eyes, but our Lord is right there, holding us close, wiping the tears away (Revelation 7:17; 21:4). I wonder if we will ever get used to the moment, a moment that will never end.

This is not just a future promise. We don't have to wait until this life is over to get a taste of the promise of heaven. When we least expect it, God surprises us by drawing us into His presence and giving us the privilege of worshipping Him. Notice I said He surprises us. You cannot schedule moments like this or put them in the bulletin for Sunday services. These are the rare opportunities we have to enjoy God's presence in such a total and complete way that we feel as though we are physically in His presence.

The moments come and go so quickly, yet as followers of Christ we know they will never truly end. Through them God gives us a preview of what heaven will be like.

The promise of heaven is not about a place. Rather, it is the promise that someday our greatest desire will be eternally satisfied—the longing to know God. Knowing God is our highest calling and our greatest privilege. His presence is *the* place where we truly know and experience all the promises He has given us. When a passion for knowing God grips us, our lives will be marked by a pursuit of God. We will not settle for substitutes, nor will we confine Him to an hour or two on Sunday mornings. Knowing God the Father becomes our greatest desire, the goal we must reach whatever the cost.

The promise of heaven also ignites a passion within us to please God. Knowing we will spend eternity with Him drives us to want to put a smile on His face. As Paul put it in his second letter to the church in Corinth:

> *Therefore, we are always confident and know that as long as we are at home in the body we are away from the Lord. We live by faith, not by sight. We are confident, I say, and would prefer to be away from the body and at home with the Lord. So we make it our goal to please him, whether we are at home in the body or away from it. For we must all appear before the judgment seat of Christ, that each one may receive what is due him for the things done while in the body, whether good or bad.* (2 Corinthians 5:6–10)

I've heard people twist these words around in such a way as to make them sound as though we must try to please the Lord in order to avoid punishment. They focus on the last sentence and paint a picture of an angry God waiting to thump us on the head if we don't do enough for Him. Who would want to serve that kind of God?

Knowing we will someday stand before the Lord should move us to act out of love, not fear. The One you and I will stand before has already taken our punishment upon Himself. When we see Him we cannot help but notice the scars on His hands and feet. Beneath His crown of glory there are the brief traces of the marks of the thorns, all reminders of His great love for us.

I don't know about you, but I don't want to stand before Him empty-handed. With all of my limited abilities and strength, I would like to do something to show Him how much I love Him. I can't do much, but I can take His gift to me of eternal life and do my best to use it for His glory. The apostle Paul's words assure me that one day God will ask me what I have done with His gift. My goal—and the goal of all of us who have tasted His mercy and grace—is to someday hear those words, "Well done, my good and faithful servant," as we cross the barrier between this life and the promise of heaven.

10

GLORY

And those he predestined, he also called;
those he called, he also justified; those he
justified, he also glorified. (*Romans 8:30*)

In the history of the world two men parted the
Red Sea, Moses and Murl Meredith. Moses we all
know about. God commanded him to lift up his
staff and see the glory of the Lord in action. Murl
took his orders from the management at Paramount
Studios. A plumber by trade, he was responsible for
devising a way to flood a huge tank with cascading
water from two sides. As the water poured in, the
cameras rolled. Cecil B. DeMille ran the film of
Murl's tank backwards, parting the Red Sea for
Charlton Heston and the rest of the cast of *The Ten
Commandments*.

By the time I became Murl's pastor, his days at
Paramount had long since passed. He never went to
the movies anymore, or to church, or anywhere else
because of the toll arthritis had taken on his body.
Every moment of every day was spent in bed. His
back and legs could no longer support his ever
shrinking weight. Murl's greatest desire wasn't to
part the Red Sea again but to see the skies parted
with Christ coming down to take him home. His
glory days didn't lie behind but ahead, for Murl
knew that his frail, weakened body would soon be

glorified. And he longed for that moment more than anything else in the world.

God promises this moment will indeed arrive. Glory is the last promise we will experience as we pass from this life. Our Lord left no doubt as to whether this long-anticipated event will occur. Romans 8 tells us that those God justified, these He also glorified. The Bible speaks of the event as though it took place in the past, even though its fulfillment lies in the future. Like all of God's promises, this one is guaranteed.

The Lord guarantees to change us with glory. These changes will be dramatic. The work God began in us on the day we said yes to Christ will be perfected. In our glorified bodies we will be totally free from sin. Morally we will be perfect, completely holy. Impure thoughts will never again plague us. All of our spiritual struggles will be over once and for all. We will be like our Lord, pure and holy and undefiled.

As we see the Lord, our knowledge will also be glorified. No longer will we see in part or gaze at a poor reflection in a mirror. On that day we will see the Lord. We will be fully known by the Lord and we will know in full. Whether or not that means that we will understand all of the mysteries of life, such as the intricate details of creation, the Bible does not say. Whatever knowledge He gives us will be enough. Even with glorified minds, there will be mysteries in heaven that will puzzle us forever. We will always wonder why God would love us so much as to send His Son to die for us. Pondering that mystery will keep us at His throne, praising Him forever.

We will be able to approach His throne, for every trace of sin's residue will be washed away. To be glorified means to be clothed in the full righteousness of Christ, to be completely justified. In God's sight we will be completely holy. No charge can be brought against one of His elect, for the full requirements of the law are met in us through Christ. When we are glorified, this process will reach its climax. No one will be able to point a finger at someone the Lord has redeemed and say, "She doesn't deserve to be here!" Instead we will be on display as an eternal testimony of the love and grace of God.

The final trumpet, signaling the end of time and life as we know it, will also usher in the climactic change we mere mortals long for—our glorified, immortal bodies.

> *Listen, I tell you a mystery: We will not all sleep, but we will all be changed—in a flash, in the twinkling of an eye, at the last trumpet. For the trumpet will sound, the dead will be raised imperishable, and we will be changed. For the perishable must clothe itself with the imperishable, and the mortal with immortality. (1 Corinthians 15:51–53)*

Our present bodies are perishable, subject to pain and disease and death. But our glorified bodies will be imperishable, free from all the ailments that make life miserable. Our present body is sown in dishonor, but our new bodies will be glorious, and they will be raised up in power. Today we wear a natural body, but someday we will be given a spiritual body made for eternity, made to spend all of its time in the presence of God (see 1 Corinthians 15:42–49).

Revelation 19:8 tells us that on the day we are glorified, God will clothe us in white robes of righteousness. Crowns will be given to us so that we can reign with Him forever (2 Timothy 4:8). As all of these things are placed upon us by Christ, we will be overwhelmed with the knowledge that we do not deserve any of them. The scene from heaven recorded in Revelation 4, where the twenty-four elders cast their crowns at the feet of Christ, will be repeated on the day we are glorified. In an act of worship, thanksgiving, and adoration, we too will cast our crowns at the feet of the One who deserves all glory. We will give glory to King Jesus, to whom we owe all things.

Part 2

PROMISES THE LORD MAKES ABOUT HIS CHARACTER AND ACTIONS

11

ATTENTION

The eyes of the Lord are on the righteous and his ears are attentive to their cry. *(Psalm 34:15)*

The man said he forgot his child was in the car. All of his friends and family rushed in to support him. He would never intentionally harm his infant son, they all testified. Quite the contrary; everyone said that he was a good father, a man devoted to his children. He simply made a mistake on the hot July day he dashed into a home improvement superstore to pick up one or two items.

No need to take the baby inside, he thought. *I'll just be gone a minute or two.* Once inside, the endless aisles of power saws and light fixtures distracted him. Before he knew it, time had slipped away from him, and his young son had been locked in a hot car for nearly twenty minutes. The Indianapolis police said that the woman who passed by the car saved the child's life. Another ten minutes or so and the child would have died. No one felt worse about the incident than the father. After all, he was a good dad. He just temporarily forgot his son.

If deciding between varying shades of taupe paint can drive the existence of one child from a father's mind, imagine what God faces every day. He has a universe to run, galaxies to keep in order, time and eternity to manage. As if that were not enough, planet Earth is filled with nearly six billion human beings, all created in His image, all demanding His time. Yet the Bible promises us that God can never forget one of His children. He does much more than remember that we are sitting in a car on a hot summer afternoon. Psalm 34 promises us that He constantly watches us. Our Lord gives us His undivided attention.

Psalm 34 and the promise it contains form one of my favorite passages in the Bible. Take a long look at the picture these words paint of God. His eyes are on the righteous (verse 15), and the previous psalm tells us why: "The eyes of the Lord are on those who fear him, on those whose hope is in his unfailing love, *to deliver them from death and keep them alive in famine*" (Psalm 33:18; italics added). The Creator and Sustainer of all of creation watches your life and mine like a father watches his child take her first steps. His hands are close by our side in order that He might immediately steady us and keep us from falling. Long before we think of crying out for help He is already there.

He not only keeps His eye on us, He is also keenly aware of everything that surrounds us. David wrote Psalm 34:15 in the middle of his darkest hour. Saul was trying to kill him, everyone had abandoned him, and David had nowhere to turn. Yet he did not despair. Instead he clung to God's promise. The attempts on his life and his painful wandering did not take the Lord by surprise.

David knew the "eyes of the Lord are on the righteous." Jesus repeated this truth in Matthew 6:25–34 when He told His disciples to stop worrying. God already knows all of our needs even before we ask. His eyes are always upon us.

And His ears are attentive to our prayer. The psalmist pictures God in heaven, waiting for us to cry out to Him. He is never too busy to listen. Our ramblings never bore Him. If we could catch a glimpse of Him with our eyes, we would never see Him absentmindedly nodding or muttering "uh-huh," as I sometimes do with my own children. When we call out to Him in prayer, He promises to give us His total, undivided attention. In fact, He encourages us to come and talk to Him about everything. "Pray continually," He tells us through Paul in 1 Thessalonians 1:17. "I am always listening, always paying attention."

I don't know how God does it. More to the point, I don't know *why* God chooses to keep an eye on me. It is not as if He doesn't have better things to do. There must be a few hundred million people more interesting and more righteous. And why would He listen for my voice? I'm sure He must grow tired of hearing the same prayers over and over, and He must be sick of me asking for help with the same problems. I get impatient with my own children in such a short time; why doesn't God grow impatient with me? Why does He watch? Why does He listen? Why does He pay attention to me?

Or to you? Or to any human being? He doesn't have to. Nothing obligates Him. If He were more like us He wouldn't listen to us or care for us. We're sinners, after all. All of us have at one time or another told Him to leave us alone. By all rights He should ignore us. It would serve us right.

God's promise of attention is like all the other promises of God. There is no logical explanation of why God would obligate Himself to listen to the cries of sinners like you and me. But grace and love aren't very logical. They cannot be explained, only appreciated by creatures of dust who do not deserve them but sorely need them. Without His attentive care, our fate would be far worse than a child locked in a car on a hot July afternoon.

12

INTIMACY

> I want to know Christ and the power of
> his resurrection and the fellowship of sharing
> in his sufferings. *(Philippians 3:10)*

There are moments in life that words cannot adequately describe. The long embrace of a husband and wife, a child sitting on her father's lap, a family passing a day together running and playing in a park. Words tell us that people are in motion but they cannot convey the depth of emotion the participants feel. Trying to capture the essence of the moments with mere letters and punctuation is not only impossible, it insults those who were there. Some emotions are too deep for words.

And so it is with the promise of God that is at the heart of the relationship He initiates with those who cling to Him by faith. God promises us through Christ a relationship of intimacy. The Bible uses many metaphors to describe this relationship. Among them is the word picture of a Father and His children, a Master and His servants, a Friend who sticks closer than a brother and lays down His life for His friends. There are pictures of a Shepherd and His sheep, a King and His subjects, and the Redeemer and the slaves He rescues from bondage.

Each picture portrays a different aspect of our association with God. But the one that fully de-

scribes the level of intimacy God made us to share
with Him is that of a bridegroom and His bride.

God made us to know Him. The same term for
know is used in the Old Testament to describe the
union of a man and woman that results in the birth
of a child. Here is the place words become inadequate. There is a level of joy and satisfaction and
peace that flows out of a love relationship between
a husband and wife that cannot be explained to
those who have not experienced it. As one hand
touches another while walking along a beach or sitting in church, something happens. Hollywood
calls it sparks, but it is far more than that. It is the
sharing of a life and a love, an intimacy that can
only be described as two becoming one flesh.

This intimacy, this oneness, goes beyond physical attraction. As time passes, the two partners can
grow to the point of fuller understanding of one another. I find that my wife and I can finish one
another's sentences if we so choose. Our thoughts
run together communicating vast ideas with nothing more than a glance. Two people who love one
another and are building a life together also find
that they enjoy nothing more than the joy of one
another's company. Nothing is held back, nor
would they ever think of holding back. To say they
know one another understates the matter.

This is the sort of relationship our God draws
us into with Himself. Throughout the Bible He declares His love for us, a love that lasts forever and
ever. Through the Old Testament prophets, He
called out to Israel and Judah, His chosen people,
and urged them to come back to Him as a bride
comes back to her husband.

When God tells us in the Scriptures what He requires of us, He doesn't start listing rules of behavior or prohibitions against certain actions. His greatest commandment, the one upon which all of the others rest, is this, "Love the Lord your God with all your heart and with all your soul and with all your strength" (Deuteronomy 6:5). Within this relationship God calls us to know Him. Not to know about Him, not to have a one-time encounter with Him, but to know Him more and more every day. He calls us to lose ourselves in Him, to praise Him, to delight ourselves in Him alone. As we draw near to Him, He promises to draw near to us, like a husband drawing his bride close to his side. In that moment He becomes more real than any human lover, as His Spirit touches ours.

The Lord makes this intimacy possible by placing His Holy Spirit within us on the day we accepted Christ as our Savior. Through His Spirit we can experience intimacy with Someone we've never met face-to-face. By His Spirit He draws us to Himself, creating within us the desire that Paul spoke of when he cried out, "I want to know Christ and the power of his resurrection and the fellowship of sharing in his sufferings" (Philippians 3:10). He makes our souls hunger and thirst with an appetite that can only be satisfied with God Himself.

And He promises to satisfy that desire. He promises to open the doors of the throne room of heaven in order that we might constantly spend time with Him. "Come near to God and he will come near to you," the Scripture declares in James 4:8. I need to warn you: When we begin to experience the fullness of this promise, our lives will never be the same.

The apostle Paul described the transformation in this way:

> But whatever was to my profit I now consider loss for the sake of Christ. What is more, I consider everything a loss compared to the surpassing greatness of knowing Christ Jesus my Lord, for whose sake I have lost all things. I consider them rubbish, that I may gain Christ. (Philippians 3:7–8)

Experiencing intimacy with Christ makes everything else in life seem unimportant. Just one moment in His embrace will make us spend the rest of our lives in pursuit of Him. God promises that as we pursue Him, we will find Him.

13

LOVE

> For I am convinced that neither death nor
> life, neither angels nor demons, neither the
> present nor the future, nor any powers,
> neither height or depth, nor anything else in
> all creation, will be able to separate us from
> the love of God that is in Christ Jesus our
> Lord. (*Romans 8:38–39*)

We mouth the words with the greatest of ease.
"I love you. I love you just the way you are."
"I will love you forever and ever." "My love is higher
than the mountains and deeper than the ocean" (or
deeper than the holler, for you country music fans).
"My love for you will never die." And we mean
what we say. Yet time always finds a way to make
our words sound hollow. In a moment of anger or
frustration or selfishness, we push the object of our
love away and we see how conditional our love really is.

Unconditional love is difficult for us to understand and nearly impossible to exercise. But God
has proven once and for all that His promise to love
is completely unconditional. As Romans 5:8 states,
"But God demonstrates his own love for us in this:
While we were still sinners, Christ died for us."
While we were still sinners—when we were at our
absolute worst—God loved us. When we had nothing to offer Him, when He was the furthest thing
from our mind, God loved us. In spite of our con-
tinuing struggle with sin, God loves us. Unconditionally, with no strings attached, He loves us.

God's love is more than words and promises. He put His love into action through Christ's death on the cross. As John 3:16 timelessly states, "For God so loved the world that he gave his one and only Son." Through death Jesus took the penalty of our sin upon Himself in order that we might be forgiven. He met our greatest need by paying the highest of all prices, the price of His own life. Why would He do such a thing? Simply because He loves us.

God's promise to love us unconditionally flows from the Cross and completely changes the way we live our lives. All of us have a tendency to question God's unconditional love for us as individuals. We wonder how He could love us even after we come to Christ. Our lives are so inconsistent. We struggle with the same old sins over and over and over again. His Word tells us to do many things that we never get around to doing. How could He love someone like you and me?

But He does, no matter what we do, or fail to do. His love for His children is not based on our performance. God doesn't love Billy Graham any more than you or me. The Bible declares that He loves us because He has chosen to love us. Nothing about us attracted Him to us and nothing about us will drive Him away. As the passage that opened this chapter states, nothing can separate us from the love of God that is in Christ Jesus our Lord.

His love also reassures us that He will never leave us or forsake us. I must admit, there have been times in my life when I tried to run away from Him. My only prayer was "Leave me alone!!" I never actually said those words out loud, but my lifestyle shouted them out. God's plan for my life had all the appeal of having a few more wisdom teeth dug out. I did not want anything to do with His plan or with Him. My rebellion did not cause Him to stop loving me. He never left me or forsook me, even when I wanted Him to. His love would not allow it.

Nor would His love leave me in the state I chose for myself. Because sin separates us from God, He removes it. The writer of the book of Hebrews tells us that God disciplines those He loves (12:6). Sometimes gently, sometimes not so gently, He breaks the hold of sin on our lives to remake us in the image of His Son. Discipline is rarely pleasant, either for the one administering or the one receiving it. But God loves us enough to give us what we need, rather than what we want.

Some still argue that God's love is not completely unconditional. They say that if God really loves everyone, He would save everyone. A loving God would guarantee every member of the human race a spot in heaven. And He wouldn't try to change us. Real love, real unconditional love, would accept us and our sin. All those narrow rules and regulations found in the Bible show us that God only loves those who keep His law and do good works.

Yet the Bible assures us that God does love everyone in the world, in spite of what they have or have not done. Jesus died as a demonstration of God's love for every human being who has been or ever will be born. But not everyone will be saved. The vast majority of the human race will reject the forgiveness the Cross offers, preferring sin to righteousness. Those who reject Him and those who never believe in Him will be separated from Him forever. Hell is made all the more tragic by the fact that God does love everyone consigned to its flames.

The truth is, God loves everyone enough to send His Son on their behalf. Those who will have a place in heaven, who will be saved, are any and all who choose to believe.

14

GUIDANCE

> As Jesus walked beside the Sea of Galilee, he saw Simon and his brother Andrew casting a net into the lake, for they were fishermen. "Come, follow me," Jesus said, "and I will make you fishers of men." At once they left their nets and followed him. (Mark 1:16–18)

All of the commands of Christ can be found in two simple words, "Follow Me." Simon and Andrew heard these words while casting their fishing net. Jesus didn't give them many details. He never drew a map in the sand outlining all of the places they would go, nor did He explain what they could expect along the way. "Follow me, and I will make you fishers of men," is all He said, and it was enough.

Later Jesus passed Levi in a tax collector's booth. Most people avoided men like Levi. He was little more than a thief empowered by the hated Roman government. None of that concerned Jesus. As He walked by He called out to Levi, "Follow me." Levi left everything and followed Christ.

Saul of Tarsus heard those words while traveling along the road to Damascus. He had to be thrown to the ground and blinded before he would listen, but once he began to follow, he never turned back.

I first heard these words as a six-year-old child at the Regency Park Baptist Church in Moore, Oklahoma. The guest speaker said a lot more, but the essential message of Christ rang through. "Follow Me." And I started on a lifelong journey.

In many ways all of the New Testament is an expansion on these two words. Through twenty-seven books we hear the full implications of what it means to follow Christ. We find why we must follow Him and the ultimate destination He has for us. The call that echoes through every book is the call to surrender our will to the will of Christ. He does not tell us where we will go; He does not tell us what to expect. "Follow Me," Jesus cries out to every generation willing to listen. Implicit within His call is a promise. If we will follow, we can rest in the knowledge that He knows where we need to go. He will guide us every step of the way throughout the rest of our lives. We don't have to worry about taking a wrong turn or getting lost. All we have to do is follow; He will guide.

I do not have the space to explore where He will take us or even how to find the perfect will of God. But we do not need to know either in order to enjoy God's promise to guide us. I am constantly amazed at God's power to take my life in His direction without my having a clue as to what is going on. More than once I took off in pursuit of what I thought was God's will, only to find He had planned a different destination entirely. Other times I have tried my best to resist Him and set my own course. For a while I think I am successful, only to find that He still manages to get me to where He wanted me to be. To be honest, I frequently don't know where He is taking me. I fret and worry and chew my fingernails, wondering where the next stop will be. But He never frets. He just leads.

I suppose it is possible for a Christian to dig in his or her heels and refuse to budge when God says it is time to move out. It is possible, but not advisable. Our way never takes us any place worth going. We run into hazards we never knew were there. God knows. That is why He doesn't leave the driving to us. Sometimes we argue with Him over His ultimate destination for our lives. We do not want to be a pastor or a missionary or a school teacher or policeman or whatever it is God has planned for our particular lives.

Usually our resistance comes from our incomplete knowledge of what He can and will do in that place. The children of Israel, for example, thought God had played a cruel trick on them when they first came to the land of Canaan. The land was full of scary giants, according to the twelve men who spied out the land. (Read the story in Numbers 13:1–14:4.) They forgot giants were no match for a much bigger God. He really knew what He was doing after all. (Two of the spies, Joshua and Caleb, recognized God's superior power, but the people still trembled [14:6–10].)

As God guides us, He still knows what He is doing. The unpleasant surprises that spring up along the way do not take Him by surprise. We want to run and hide, but the Lord calls back to us to keep on trusting, keep on following. Other times we want to settle down in a place the Lord says we are just passing through. We wonder why we can't stay longer, but He doesn't answer. All He says is the same thing He said to the fishermen along the shore of the Sea of Galilee, "Follow Me. I know where I am going."

15

GRACE

Three times I pleaded with the Lord to take it [the thorn in my flesh] away from me. But he said to me, "My grace is sufficient for you, for my power is made perfect in weakness." (*2 Corinthians 12:8–9*)

Three times the apostle Paul prayed the same prayer and three times he received the same answer. It was not the answer he was hoping to hear. Something was tormenting Paul. He never said what it was, though he called it a "thorn in my flesh," a messenger of Satan sent to make his life miserable. And it was succeeding. "Take it away from me," he pleaded with the Lord, but the thorn never went away.

"My grace is sufficient for you, for my power is made perfect in weakness," was all the Lord would say. As the thorn wore Paul down, God's grace became stronger. When Paul reached his breaking point, he could see why God had allowed this trial to strike. Rather than give up, Paul rejoiced, for God's grace made him strong in his hour of greatest weakness.

In the introduction I spoke of how easy it is to take God's promises for granted. We get so caught up in our daily activities that we hardly give a thought to all that God is doing in us and around us. The invisible hardly registers on our radar screens, causing us to conclude that He must not

be there, or if He is, He is keeping to Himself. This
is especially true of the promise of God's grace. We
think a lot of His grace when we contemplate the
fact that He saved us. Salvation comes as a gift of
God's grace.

The promise of God's grace stretches beyond
the moment of salvation to encompass all of God's
dealings with believers. Without God's grace we
would be nothing. Without His grace we could do
nothing. As Paul discovered in his struggle with his
thorn in the flesh, God's grace transforms our
weakness into His strength. Grace gives us help in
our time of need as well as bestows upon us everything we need to fulfill God's plan for our lives. The
fact that God has a plan and a calling for us flows
from His grace.

For those who profess to follow Christ by faith,
everything comes down to the grace of God.

To fully appreciate the grace of God, we need
to consider where we would be without it. By His
grace God gives us what we do not deserve, so let
us consider for a moment what life would be like if
He gave us what we deserved. The root of the word
grace means "to give, a gift." Let's suppose God did
not give gifts but paid us the wages we have earned.
The result can hardly be called life.

You and I are sinners. We like to do things that
displease God and destroy ourselves. The essence
of sin is selfishness. *Leave me alone; let me do what I
want to do,* is the motto of selfish people, of sinners
like you and me. If God gave us what we deserved,
He would leave us alone. Completely alone. He
would let us fend for ourselves as we try to survive
in a harsh world. We wouldn't survive long. The

Bible tells us that the air we breathe and the rain that gives life both are gifts of God (see Zechariah 10:1). Without His grace, life would cease to exist.

Not that we would want to exist very long without Him. God made us to know Him. Deep within our souls is a hunger that can only be satisfied by God Himself. If God gave us what we deserved in payment for our sin, He would block the path back to Him forever. He would never speak; He would never intervene in the affairs of mankind. Prayer would not exist, for He would not listen to what we have to say. We would finally have what people have been asking for since the beginning of time: life without God. But it would be a lonely existence indeed. It wouldn't be life. The Bible calls it eternal death. It already exists in a place the Bible calls hell, which just happens to be the wages we deserve for our sin.

Instead of giving us what we deserve, God's grace promises everything we never dreamed could be ours. By God's grace He offers forgiveness and new life. By His grace we can be justified freely through the redemption that came by Christ Jesus, Paul declares in Romans 3:24. This same grace breaks the power of sin in our lives. Sin will not be the master of those who are under grace (Romans 6:14). By God's grace we now have access to the very presence of God. Hebrews 4:16 calls God's throne the throne of grace, a place we can go anytime we want to receive help in our time of need. Because of His incomprehensible grace, God displays His power in our times of weakness.

Grace both gives us life and makes life worth living. Whenever the apostle Paul talked about his role as a missionary and apostle, he always gave the credit to the grace of God that called him into that ministry. The same grace at work in Paul's life is at work in your life and mine. It pulls us out of a wasted existence and makes our life into something that will bear fruit for eternity. Not only does God's grace call us, it gives us the power to fulfill His calling and do His will. It expresses itself to us by calling us to serve Him in specific ways.

The promise of God's grace is the promise of His unmerited favor. His grace is always sufficient, no matter how sharp the thorns in our flesh may be.

16

COMPLETION

He who began a good work in you will carry it on to completion until the day of Christ Jesus. *(Philippians 1:6)*

I was a self-made man. I worked hard developing my character, refining my vocabulary, polishing the qualities that were me. I carefully selected traits from people I admired and made them my own; I crafted the image I wanted everyone else to see; I made all the decisions and took all the credit for the finished product. I was a self-made man, and was proud of it. All that I was I owed to myself.

Funny, I would rather not go into much detail about the specific qualities that radiated from the person who was Mark Tabb. This self-made man who was so proud of who he had become now feels nothing but shame at the memory.

I'm no longer a self-made man. Someone else took over the job. Someone who knows what He is doing. Someone who stubbornly refuses to give up until the job is finished.

His work is cut out for Him because His biggest obstacle is the self-made man that I carefully crafted. Everything I did must be undone, torn down, put to death. Everything. All of it is worthless. Nothing is worth salvaging. He has to start over from scratch.

I don't know why He took on such a monu-
mental task. From my viewpoint I cannot see that
He has anything to gain. Many days I put up so
much resistance that He probably feels like He is
wasting His time. But He keeps right on working,
tearing down the old, building the new.

He has been working a long time. A very long
time. I would have stopped long ago, but not Him.
Not my God. He promises to finish the work that
He began in my life on the day He saved me, even if
it takes until the end of time. And it will. But He
doesn't care. In His eyes the finished product is
worth the time and the effort.

Before He started, my life made Him turn away
in disgust. Now He is remaking me and everyone
else who names the name of Christ in the image of
His Son. This is the promise of completion. He will
complete His work in me; He will develop me into
the person He wants me to become. Theologians
refer to this as *sanctification*, the process where God
sets us apart to His purpose and His glory. He already calls us *saints* or *holy ones*; now He is working
to make this term true in our daily lives. His goal is
to transform you and me into people whose lives
will please Him in every way.

According to Colossians 1, His plans include
making us into a people whose lives are constantly

> . . . *bearing fruit in every good work, growing in the
> knowledge of God, being strengthened with all power ac-
> cording to his glorious might so that you may have great
> endurance and patience, and joyfully giving thanks to
> the Father, who has qualified you to share in the inheri-
> tance of the saints in the kingdom of light. For he has*

> *rescued us from the dominion of darkness and brought*
> *us into the kingdom of the Son he loves. (Colossians*
> *1:10–13)*

With God on the job, He will make sure that
we bear fruit, that our knowledge of Him increases,
that we grow stronger in grace, and that we walk in
thanksgiving to God. Those are not ideals or unat-
tainable goals we are supposed to shoot for. Rather,
God uses them as a blueprint to reshape our lives.
He starts the process on the day He rescues us from
the dominion of darkness and brings us into the
kingdom of the Son He loves—on the day we accept Christ as our Savior. Far too often we see that
day as the climax of God's work in our lives. Our
Lord sees it as the starting point of a process He
promises to complete.

All of this poses some problems for a man like
me who once worked so hard trying to make himself complete. It makes me realize that I have very
little to contribute to the process. God doesn't want
or need my suggestions for fine-tuning my life. He
doesn't need my help nor is He helping *me* put my
life in order. As much as I hate to admit it, He is doing it all. Every bit. My single contribution, the
only thing I can do to help the process along, is to
die to self and follow Him by faith. Paul said it best
in Galatians 2:20, "I have been crucified with
Christ and I no longer live, but Christ lives in me.
The life I live in the body, I live by faith in the Son
of God."

This creates an even greater dilemma for someone who took such pride in being a self-made man:
All that I am and all that I will ever be I owe to Him.

Any good in me and any good works I may accomplish come from God. The positive changes in my life over the course of the past two decades are His handiwork, not mine. I cannot take credit for anything, nor would I ever think of doing so. I owe everything to Him. And so do you.

He's not finished yet. We do not know what the next few days or decades will hold. My life and yours are works in progress. Thankfully we have His promise that He will never settle for anything less than perfection. The work He started He will carry through to completion.

RETURN

> "Men of Galilee," they said, "why do you stand here looking into the sky? This same Jesus, who has been taken from you into heaven, will come back in the same way you have seen him go into heaven." *(Acts 1:11)*

He was gone. Vanished into the clouds. They assumed He would stay with them forever. Forty days earlier they had felt unspeakable joy when they learned He walked out of the tomb. Now, just when they thought that He was ready to usher in His kingdom, He disappeared into heaven. All they could do was stand and stare into the sky in shock.

"Men of Galilee, why do you stand here looking into the sky?" They must have felt foolish by the rebuke. The angels assumed that Peter and John and the rest understood Jesus' plan when He told them to wait in Jerusalem for the promise of the Holy Spirit. Once they received the Spirit, they were to take the gospel to the world. Jesus never hid the fact that He would leave them. After He was gone, they were to finish the work He began. The angels reminded them that He would return, just as He had promised (John 14:3). Until that time the disciples had a job to do.

Two thousand years have passed since Jesus departed. The small group who watched Him depart has multiplied a million times over. What was once a small band of Jewish believers now encompasses people from every inhabited continent and racial group. The promise that Jesus made and the angels repeated applies to us all. This same Jesus who disappeared into the clouds over the hills of Judea—who went to prepare a home for us—will return in the same way. And He will return for us.

The world hardly has room for the books devoted to the subject of His promised return. Knowing He will return is not enough for most of us. We want details. We want to know when. And how. And where. We want to know the signs and the seasons and how current events fit into His prophetic calendar. Through the years the angels' words have become more puzzle than promise. We want to crack the code and discover the date.

In our efforts to solve the puzzle, multiple eschatological systems have developed. We have pre-tribs and post-tribs and mid-tribs. There are pre-mills and post-mills and no-mills; historicists and futurists, and it-will-all-pan-out-in-the-end-icists. Not recognizing the terms only means you have a lot to learn. And you better learn it. There could be a test later.

Believers today know more about the ins and outs of the Lord's return, but most of us are doing little more than standing alongside the disciples, staring into the sky as we try to understand the signs of the times. Jesus told His disciples not to worry about times or dates regarding the coming of His kingdom. He wasn't being coy. When He discussed His return, He wasn't giving clues to prophetic sleuths.

All we need to know is the promise: He will return. We do not know when, we do not know any other details. But He is coming back. He gave us His word.

And He gave us a task to do in the meantime. After His longest discourse on His return, Jesus told a story about a servant whose master left him in charge of the house while he traveled. The story is found in Matthew 24:45–51. The master returned to find his servant faithfully carrying out his duties. In reward the master put the servant in charge of his entire estate. But Jesus warned of consequences if the master had found his house in disrepair and the servant partying. The master of that servant would assign him to a place of weeping and gnashing of teeth.

Jesus' story reminds us that before He returned to His Father, He entrusted us with the task of taking the gospel to the world. "You will receive power when the Holy Spirit comes on you; and you will be my witnesses . . . to the ends of the earth" (Acts 1:8). The ends of the earth begin next door. We are surrounded by people whose only exposure to the name Jesus comes when they drop a hammer on their toe. Our Lord left us here to tell everyone about Him. The time we have to carry out this task is limited, for the work must stop when He returns. In the meantime we should be filled with urgency. The time is short; the size and scope of our task is almost overwhelming. We don't have a moment to spare.

His promised return also reminds us that our lives count for something when we devote ourselves to the work of the Lord. The apostle Paul concluded his letter to the church in Corinth with a reminder of Jesus' promise to return and these words, "Always give yourselves fully to the work of the Lord, because you know that your labor in the Lord is not in vain" (1 Corinthians 15:58). When Christ returns, He will bring along His reward for those who love Him, those who longed for His appearing, and those who were faithful to His task. The only way to be ready for His return is to be busy completing the work we have received in the Lord (Colossians 4:17).

May the Lord come soon.

18

JUSTICE

> [The wicked] have no struggles; their bodies are healthy and strong. They are free from the burdens common to man; they are not plagued by human ills. . . . This is what the wicked are like—always carefree, they increase in wealth. . . . When I tried to understand all this, it was oppressive to me till I entered the sanctuary of God; then I understood their final destiny. *(Psalm 73:4–5, 12, 16–17)*

He's right, you know. Asaph, the guy who wrote the words above, is right. Somewhere along the line, we picked up the mistaken idea that God always blesses the righteous and punishes the wicked. I see a lot of people who qualify as wicked in the eyes of God, people who wouldn't be caught dead inside a church, people who snicker at the idea of prayer, people who couldn't care less about God, and people who make fun of the Bible and those who read it. They are everywhere. Life seems to be pretty good for them. I try to convince myself that they are not really happy because they do not know the Lord, but some of them do a pretty good imitation of happy people. They smile and laugh a lot while they do all those things God-fearing people won't do.

Asaph is exactly right. The wicked have no struggles. Their bodies are healthy and strong. They don't worry about getting caught when they exercise creativity in filling out their tax forms. I know they deal with stress, but so do I. They have

the advantage, for they don't have the added stress
of trying to please God. They ignore Him and scoff
at His laws. Shouldn't a lightning bolt give them a
good shock right about now? Lightning bolts don't
frighten them, nor does God. They assume He has
to let them into heaven.

Preach it, Asaph. Amen, brother. Life is *not* fair.
People do anything they please these days and get
away with it. The rich and the famous and the guy
down the street are having way too much fun in
life. "Surely in vain have I kept my heart pure; in
vain have I washed my hands in innocence" (Psalm
73:13). I feel like that sometimes too. *Why keep the
rules when those who bend them always get ahead?
Nice guys finish last.* Just thinking about all this
makes my stomach hurt.

Looking at the world through the eyes of the
world will always get us down. Truth and justice
and fairness don't stand a chance in the win-at-any-
cost culture in which we live. But we aren't supposed
to look at the world through the eyes of the world.
When we, like Asaph, get around to seeing life from
God's perspective, everything changes: "I entered
the sanctuary of God; then I understood their final
destiny" (verse 17).

God promises to bring about justice someday.
In the end He will have the final say as to who wins
and who loses. On that day, justice will win. Everyone will get exactly what he deserves.

Without the promise of justice we would not
be able to live by faith very long. The huge questions about good and evil would rob us of our
strength and cause us to walk away, accusing God
of being less than God. Without the promise of jus-

tice, the actions of men like Joseph Stalin would silence everything we say we believe. He was evil incarnate. History shows that more people died at the hand of Stalin than Hitler. The oppression and terror he unleashed never compelled the armies of the world to take action.

Stalin remained defiant until the day of his death, ordering the execution of his enemies even to the very end. One day, however, Joseph Stalin will stand before God and get what he deserves. One day every wicked person who chose pleasure over God will stand before Him, and justice will prevail. One day every person who has ever lived will stand before God, and justice will be served.

On this side of eternity the world seems out of whack. Evil advances while justice retreats. Cheaters win and those who play by the rules lose. Do not fret. God has established a day when He will judge the world with righteousness. In the end His justice will triumph.

Before we take too much pleasure in the thought that evil people will get what is coming to them someday, we need to remember that we too qualify as evil in God's eyes. Romans 3:23 reminds us that we all have sinned and fall short of the glory of God. Men like Joseph Stalin may be monsters in our sight, but when we stand before the Lord, we will be just as guilty. Every one of us has rebelled against God. We have all tried to kick Him off His throne. The original sin consisted of trying to be God rather than submit to Him. I must admit that I am guilty as charged.

God's justice should mean punishment for every person; yet the promise of justice amplifies the glory of God's grace. Through the Cross God maintains His justice while opening the door for mercy. Christ took our punishment upon Himself. He received what we deserve, in order that we can receive what we could never earn: forgiveness and mercy. This same Jesus who died upon the cross is the One who will bring justice with Him when He returns. Every man, woman, and child who has ever drawn a breath will stand before Him to be judged. No one can cry out for an appeal or question the fairness of the verdict. On that day every tongue will be silenced; everyone will know that God has been fair with them. Justice will prevail.

Asaph understood the final destiny of the wicked; so should we. God sent His Son to die for the world in order that that destiny might change. What are we willing to do?

19

CONSISTENCY

"I the Lord do not change." *(Malachi 3:6)*

I faced a minor crisis this week. A problem arose and I didn't know what to do. My first response was to take a couple of Advils. Worrying about the problem gave me a headache. Then I tried to plot a way through the crisis of the moment. I schemed and planned and plotted strategy. But my best-laid plans only made matters worse. Time to swallow more Advil. I tried moaning and complaining, but that only made the people around me take a few steps back.

Finally I tried praying. I meant to pray sooner, as a first resort rather than a last, but worrying and scheming and complaining come so naturally that prayer gets pushed back.

The crisis ended today. God came through. He answered prayer and intervened in human affairs. His plan is perfect; His timing impeccable.

Looking at how effortlessly He managed to solve a dilemma that cost me several nights' sleep, I am in awe. I can hardly believe what He has done. To be honest, I guess I am surprised. God came through —how shocking. He answered prayer and put His plan into action, and I was surprised. Surprised by God.

Why should I be? God did what He always does. His actions in my life this week were no different than what He did four thousand years ago in the life of Abraham or two thousand years ago in the life of Paul or fifty years ago in the life of my grandfather. He was faithful to His promises, faithful to His Word, faithful to His children. "The one who calls you is faithful and he will do it," Paul wrote of our consistent, unchanging God (1 Thessalonians 5:24). And still, to see Him in action, I find myself surprised.

And so do you. Listen to our stories at church. We all act amazed when God answers prayers and proves Himself to be faithful. In some ways we should be amazed. We never want to become so accustomed to God's grace that we take Him for granted. Yet our surprise shows how little we understand about the character of God. He promises to be the same yesterday, today, and forever. He promises to be consistent.

Maybe that is why we are so surprised when God acts just as He has always acted. He is always consistent; we rarely are. We're always changing our minds; He never does. Like politicians, we constantly reinvent ourselves; God stays the same forever. From our clothes to our slang, we constantly struggle to stay up-to-date; He is completely unaffected by time. His Word will stand forever. He never changes.

Think what life would be like if He did change —if God were more like us. What would happen if tomorrow He decided that He was tired of the

sound of our voices and He shut down the hot line
of prayer? What would our lives be like if He decided that faith in Christ was no longer enough with
Him, and we had to prove ourselves worthy of His
love? Who could stop Him if He decided to add a
few hundred new commands to His law, commands modeled after the United States tax codes?
Imagine you awoke tomorrow and discovered that
He had outlawed sports or chocolate or the use of
the letter "Y" while we slept. How unbearable life
would be if God were as inconsistent and as capricious as you and I.

Thankfully, God is not like us. He declares in
Malachi 3:6, "I the Lord do not change. So you, O
descendants of Jacob, are not destroyed." Everything He does is always consistent with His
character and holiness. He cannot and will not vio-
late His moral attributes. Because God will always
be consistent with Himself, we can be assured that
He will never tempt us to sin (James 1:13). When
assorted unexpected trials strike our lives, we know
that God is not playing games with us. He never
treats us like playthings, nor does He manipulate
our lives just for kicks. Everything He does will always reflect His absolute holiness and perfection.

God also stays consistent to His eternal purpose and plan for the universe. Revelation 13:8
describes Jesus as the Lamb that was slain from the
creation of the world. The first chapter of Ephesians assures believers that God chose us in Christ
before the foundation of the world. Both of these
statements would seem very strange if God were
constantly thinking of new ways for us to approach
Him. But He has always had one way by which

people can be saved. God's eternal purpose for the universe has always revolved around His Son and the Cross. During Old Testament times people were saved through faith as they looked forward to the Cross; today we are saved as we look back at the Cross. God's consistency shines forth as His plan for the human race never changes.

Nor does His Word change. It stands forever (1 Peter 1:25). This promise means much more than the fact that God's Word never goes through a rewrite. Every command, every law, every word, is always consistent with the essential character of God. His commands are never arbitrary words designed to control our lives. They all flow out of who God is. He never violates Himself.

God Himself declared, "I the Lord do not change" (Malachi 3:6). It shouldn't surprise us, then, when we see God act just as He always has. But it does. And it always will, for the most surprising consistency in God is His unfailing love for creatures of dust who do not deserve it.

20

SOVEREIGNTY

"Praise be to You, O Lord, God of our father Israel, from everlasting to everlasting. Yours, O Lord, is the greatness and the power and the glory and the majesty and the splendor, for everything in heaven and earth is yours. Yours, O Lord, is the kingdom; you are exalted as head over all." *(1 Chronicles 29:10–11)*

I'm watching television, minding my own business, when a show comes on about a giant asteroid that falls down from the sky and wipes out Kansas City. (Only it never blew up Kansas City. I think maybe it blew up Dallas, but that came on the second night which I did not watch because the Monkees' reunion show was on.) Part one of the asteroid movie was mildly entertaining. Lots of things blew up, which everyone knows is the sign of a good movie. The show ends and I grab the remote to turn off my television when the newscaster breaks in and starts talking about the odds of a giant asteroid coming down and wiping out my hometown of Indianapolis. It seems that one asteroid, and maybe more, have already hit the earth. They say the last one killed all the dinosaurs and the next one will destroy life as we know it.

And then I try to go to bed.

But I can't sleep. I keep thinking that at any moment a four-mile-wide chunk of planet could come sweeping down out of the heavens at thirty-four thousand miles an hour and land on my house.

And even if a giant chunk of cosmic rock doesn't land on my house, a fifty-pound block of ice might. It happened to someone in New Jersey. This man and woman were sitting in their living room watching wrestling on TV when a block of frozen drinking water from a passing airplane crashed through their roof.

And if the fifty-pound block of ice doesn't crash through my roof, I'm still not out of the woods. What if a fire breaks out in my basement? Or what if a burglar breaks in and steals my collection of Wheaties boxes? Or what if a tornado comes sweeping down the plain and sweeps me down the plain with it? Or what if the windchill drops to minus sixty-four degrees and my dog runs off again and I go outside looking for it and the door accidentally closes behind me and locks me out of the house, wearing nothing but my pajamas, and no one finds me until morning, by which time I am a one-hundred-seventy-five-pound block of ice?

And even if none of these things happens, I'm still not safe. What if the chicken I fixed for dinner had deadly bacteria crawling all over it and I didn't scrub long enough with antibacterial soap? What if I cooked it too long and the black char on the edge contained a carcinogenic and because I ate it I will develop tumors twenty years from now? But that may not matter because I was exposed to secondhand cigarette smoke at Wendy's a few weeks back. And even if the secondhand smoke doesn't get me, the electromagnetic field generated by my computer could be deadly because electromagnetic fields may be linked to a cancer cluster outside of Merced, California. And I spend a lot of time on my computer, playing my favorite arcade game, a game called Asteroids, which reminds me of the movie which started keeping me awake in the first place.

Or I can roll over and go to sleep, safe in the knowledge that nothing in the universe is so big that it can knock God off of His throne. He is sovereign over heaven and earth. A sparrow cannot fall to the ground apart from His will, much less a chunk of celestial rock. When He speaks, the universe must obey. When He marches on the earth, the mountains melt like wax. Nothing compares to the Lord. Our minds cannot comprehend His glorious power.

God is still on His throne, even if a giant asteroid does fall through my roof. God is so big and so powerful and so sovereign that He can take the worst the world can dish out and use it for His glory. Romans 8:28 reminds us, "And we know that in all things God works for the good of those who love him, who have been called according to his purpose." All things are not good. Yet not even our darkest nightmares coming true takes Him by surprise. He simply reworks what the world intended for evil and uses it for His eternal purposes.

The world is a big, bad, scary place. I'm glad God is bigger.

Part 3

PROMISES THAT SET
BELIEVERS' LIVES
APART FROM THE WORLD

21

FREEDOM

It is for freedom that Christ has set us free. Stand firm, then, and do not let yourselves be burdened again by a yoke of slavery. (*Galatians 5:1*)

Most people live with the mistaken notion that God hates fun. We look up toward heaven and see nothing more than a cosmic killjoy, an almighty being who has trouble relaxing, the ultimate negative Nelly. When we think of His Word, many of us think of it as a series of prohibitions and shall nots. If there is something we want to do, especially something we might actually enjoy, we think, He must have a rule against it. He wants us all to be a bunch of straightlaced people who don't do anything but go to church and read the Bible. Indeed, many Christians, and most non-Christians, think that God's plan for the human race is life in a box, covered with restrictions.

The Bible paints a different picture entirely. From the early pages of Scripture we find that freedom is at the heart of God's plan for you and me. His first three words to Adam (and indirectly to Eve) were, "You are free. . . ." The rest of the sentence informed them that they were free to eat the fruit of every tree and plant on the planet except one. Imagine it. They could enjoy every good thing the world had to offer without worrying about de-

stroying the environment or putting a hole in the
ozone layer. From avocados to zucchini, if a plant
produced it, they could eat it, with only one exception. The whole world lay at their feet to go out and
enjoy in perfect communion with God. As if that
were not enough, God planted a garden paradise
and dropped the first couple into it. "You are free,"
He told them, but they threw their freedom away in
exchange for bondage to sin.

A few thousand years later Moses showed the
human race how to break the bondage. Today,
those of us who take the time to wade through the
commands and regulations God gave through the
old prophet usually come away overwhelmed by all
God made the Israelites do. Yet we fail to see how
liberating the first five books of the Bible were to
those who first heard their words. God wasn't trying to put Israel in a box. Far from it. Through the
Law they could be free from the superstitious ritu-
als that marked the nations around them. They
didn't have to wonder who God was or what He required. The Law spelled it all out. It showed them
how to stay away from the grotesque sins that offended God. More than anything, the Law showed
them the way back to a living relationship with the
Lord. The heart of the Law is, "Love the Lord your
God with all your heart and with all your soul and
with all your strength" (Deuteronomy 6:5).

The ancient Israelites never quite got it. Neither do we. Jesus said His truth would set us free
(John 8:32). But we vacillate between turning freedom into a license to sin, and running away from
our freedom in fear. The church in Corinth fell into
the first extreme. They used freedom as an excuse

to indulge in practices Hollywood won't even mention. The churches of Galatia ran to the other extreme. They took sin so seriously that they surrendered their freedom in exchange for a strict legal code. Paul had to remind them in Galatians 5:1 that "it is for freedom that Christ has set us free." Two thousand years have not resulted in a firmer grip on freedom. The same two extremes, license and legalism, prevail in churches today. All the while God wants us to live the promise of freedom.

To be free in Christ means to be free from both sin and the Law. When Jesus rose from the dead, He forever broke the power of sin over those who follow Him. The stains of our guilt have been washed away. No longer do we live under the fear of death and judgment. Jesus already tasted both for us in order that we might be righteous in God's sight. The mistakes of our past no longer matter. He gives us a fresh start. Through the Holy Spirit that He pours out on every believer, we can now live free from the old habits of sin and the endless cycle of frustration which trying to keep His commands inevitably brings. As we read the Law we realize that we could never do everything it required. Christ has set us free from having to try, for He fulfilled all of the Law for us. Now, through living by the Spirit, we will not gratify the desires of the flesh (see Galatians 5:16). Our lives will reflect the holiness of God.

Ultimately, the promise of freedom is about much more than avoiding sin or even doing good works. Christ sets us free in order that we might enjoy Him. Those who call out to Him by faith are free to enter His presence whenever they please.

God created us to know Him. In Christ He sets us free from everything that separates us from Him. We don't have to wait for Him to clear His calendar; we never have to make an appointment. In every minute of every day we are free to walk with Him, to simply enjoy being near Him. No more fear of rejection, no more wasting time on things that do not matter; real freedom draws us into His presence.

Once we enter, we find that we are now free from having to prove ourselves. Instead we can die to ourselves and lose our lives in Him. As we hear His commands, we are free to obey out of our deep love for Him. It's life the way God meant it to be, set free in perfect fellowship with the Author of life.

22

PEACE

> Do not be anxious about anything, but in everything, by prayer and petition, with thanksgiving, present your requests to God. And the peace of God, which transcends all understanding, will guard your hearts and your minds in Christ Jesus. *(Philippians 4:6–7)*

Every day he talks and talks and talks, and every day it is the same test of endurance. From eight to five he gripes and complains and whines about his wife and his children and his car and his house and his neighborhood and his job. Nothing is ever good enough. No one ever treats him right. The world is out to get him. Day after day he talks, and day after day you find yourself stuck next to this coworker, the target of his negative barrage. You've requested transfers to other parts of the warehouse, but nothing ever opens up. Once or twice you've contemplated finding a new job, but the monthly mortgage payment chases those thoughts from you mind.

Driving to work your attitude starts to turn sour until you remember the promise Jesus gave His disciples. *I have told you these things, so that in me you may have peace. In this world you will have trouble. But take heart! I have overcome the world.*

Late at night you wonder how you fell into this trap. It's not like you went out and ran up a huge credit card balance on luxury items. But now the mail carrier often delivers more bills and threaten-

ing letters from creditors. Living paycheck to paycheck leaves little room for error—or leaks in the
roof. Then the washing machine breaks down, one
of the kids needs braces, and a math error on your
1040 tax return changes your refund into a deficit.
Before you know it you are two months behind on
the car payment, living in fear of foreclosure. As
your stomach begins to grind and you wonder how
you can stand another week of this stress, you remember Jesus made a promise about times like
these: "I have told you these things, so that in me
you may have peace. In this world you will have
trouble. But take heart! I have overcome the
world."

When they first wheeled her back toward the
operating room, the doctors said the procedure
would take only an hour, maybe an hour and a half
at the most. That was three hours ago. Waiting
rooms throw weights on the hands of a clock and
slow time to a crawl. The volume on the nearby
television is far too loud. No one is watching it, but
no one gets up to turn it down or turn it off. You
glance at your watch and wonder. And wait. Then
you begin thumbing through the Gideon Bible on
the table, and your eyes fall upon a promise in the
sixteenth chapter of John's gospel. You think Jesus
had you in mind: "I have told you these things, so
that in me you may have peace. In this world you
will have trouble. But take heart! I have overcome
the world" (John 16:33).

In this world we *will* have trouble. In Jesus we
can have peace. Peace that transcends our ability to
understand, peace that fills our darkest moments,
the peace of God brought by the God of peace. The

peace of God is not some fuzzy feeling that comes over us but an overwhelming assurance that God is in control. Philippians 4:5–9 sums up the promise in this way:

> *The Lord is near. Do not be anxious about anything, but in everything, by prayer and petition, with thanksgiving, present your requests to God. And the peace of God, which transcends all understanding, will guard your hearts and your minds in Christ Jesus. Finally, brothers, whatever is true, whatever is noble, whatever is right, whatever is pure, whatever is lovely, whatever is admirable—if anything is excellent or praiseworthy—think about such things. Whatever you have learned or received or heard from me, or seen in me—put it into practice. And the God of peace will be with you.*

His peace will never make it down from heaven and into our lives until we do what Paul encourages us to do in the passage you just read. First, rather than worrying, we must pray. Do not be anxious for anything; pray about everything. Worry and anxiety rob us of our peace. They focus our attention on the enormity of our problems and chase away all hope. Prayer focuses our attention on the greatness of our God and puts every problem in its proper perspective. As we pray we must place everything that troubles us in the hands of God. Trust Him. He knows what needs to be done.

And think about the things of God rather than the things of the world. "Whatever is true, whatever is noble, whatever is right, whatever is pure, whatever is lovely, whatever is admirable—if anything is excellent or praiseworthy—think about such things," Paul tells us. As you shift your attention away from the world and onto God, you will find that "the God of peace will be with you." Imagine. Both the peace of God and the God of peace will fill our hearts and minds no matter what we go through.

As we pour out our troubles to the Lord and focus our attention on the wonder of all He has done, His peace comes over us. Rather than our being swept away by worry, the peace of God guards our hearts and minds. Like a wall around a city, peace surrounds us with the very presence of God.

When coworkers test our faith, the peace of God fills our hearts. When the fear of the unknown splashes up around our heads, the peace of God keeps us afloat. When financial pressure grows unbearable, the peace of God is there for the asking. In the midst of a stormy world, God promises peace.

23

JOY

You have made known to me the path of life; you will fill me with joy in your presence, with eternal pleasures at your right hand. *(Psalm 16:11)*

The idea strikes me as scandalous. It goes against everything ingrained since birth in those of us born in America after the last world war. All our lives we have heard that the loftiest goal and the greatest good is happiness. Happiness is more than a goal; we see it as a right. The founding fathers guaranteed us life, liberty, and the pursuit of happiness. Guaranteed it. And pursue it we will. Whatever it takes to make us happy is not only desirable, but virtuous. "But it makes me happy" is *the* final word that closes every debate and justifies every action.

That is why I have so much trouble believing the scandalous truth I stumbled over the other day. Thumbing through the pages of the New Testament, I was struck by the fact that God does not carve out a safe place in the world to shelter me from everything that makes me unhappy. Death, grief, hardships, trials, even persecution will catch me in their snare someday, and God does nothing to prevent it. Moments of happiness come, but they are just that, moments. Ants invade the picnic, rain washes out the second game of the baseball doubleheader, the

snow plows open the roads and we have to take
that algebra test after all. And God stands idly by,
sensing our frustration, knowing we are unhappy,
but He doesn't do anything.

Why can't He be a little more like Mary Pop-
pins and make every day a jolly holiday? He could
do it. After all, He is God. He can do anything and
everything He wants. All He would have to do is
will it and we would have more paycheck and less
month, more laughter and fewer tears, more ice
cream and less Brussels sprouts, more weekends
and fewer Mondays. He could do it.

But He won't.

Following Christ and living by His promises
has very little to do with our own personal happiness. He never promises to make us happy, at least
not in our usual human understanding of happiness. As we shall see in later chapters, trials and
tribulations and sorrow and heartache are everyday
parts of the Christian life. Before we pull the covers
over our heads in depression, we need to see that,
while God does not make provision for human
happiness, He does something greater. Instead of
happiness, God promises to give us joy. Joy func-
tions on a level far above the temporary circum-
stance that make us happy for a short time.

The Bible paints a curious picture of joy. We
find it separated from the sort of circumstances we
usually associate with happiness. Surprisingly, the
source of all joy is a place no one would ever think
to look—a cross. The Scripture tells us, "Let us fix
our eyes on Jesus, the author and perfecter of our
faith, who for the joy set before him endured the
cross, scorning its shame, and sat down at the right

hand of the throne of God" (Hebrews 12:2). While on the cross—while suffering as a criminal and enduring the pain and humiliation of death—Jesus set His eyes on the joy set before Him.

On the cross Jesus experienced joy. I've scratched my head over that statement many times. How could the most painful instrument of torture ever conceived by man bring joy to the Son of God?

Joy is not the product of our surroundings but flows out of living in the center of God's will. Jesus found joy in the cross, the joy of obedience to the Father, and the joy of redeeming you and me from sin. As we lose our will to the will of God, we will find Christ's joy overflowing into our lives. So much of what we thought would make us happy in our natural sinful state revolved around ourselves and satisfying our appetites. In Christ we find that our greatest joy is found in sacrificing all our desires on the cross and allowing God's desires to fill our hearts.

The joy God promises goes beyond mere emotions. That is why the psalmist could write, "You have filled my heart with greater joy than when their grain and new wine abound" (Psalm 4:7), even though he cried out in the first verse of the same psalm, "Give me relief from my distress." For the Christian, real joy is rooted in the Lord's victory in the Cross and looks forward to the day Christ will take us home to be with Him. It looks beyond the present state of suffering or sorrow to see God's hand at work. And we know that He is at work. He takes everything, no matter how horrible it may be, and uses it for His eternal purpose (Romans 8:28). James assures us that the darkest trials are nothing more than God's refining fire leading us to maturity.

Several years after the Cross another man found out how real the joy of Christ could be. The apostle Paul was thrown into jail for preaching the gospel. There he sat, not knowing what his future held. At any moment he could be sentenced to death. While in his cell he wrote a letter urging the church in Philippi to "rejoice in the Lord always." He hadn't lost his mind. Rather, he had experienced the joy that flows from walking in God's will and resting in His sovereignty. Paul knew his prison term didn't take God by surprise. Instead, Paul saw how his chains caused the gospel to spread even more.

Joy is a promise and a gift, a gift we must put into action. Paul told the church in Thessalonica to "be joyful always" (1 Thessalonians 5:16). We cannot be happy always, but that isn't what we are commanded to do. By faith we choose to rejoice regardless of what life throws at us. Like peace, joy demands that we pray about everything rather than worry. Joy also moves us to give thanks in anything and everything.

Such joy cannot flow out of ourselves nor can it be mustered up with an incredible amount of willpower. Rather, joy flows from the Holy Spirit and fills our soul as a promise from God. As we choose to rejoice we receive the promise by faith and put it into action.

24

PURPOSE

For we are God's workmanship, created in Christ Jesus to do good works, which God prepared in advance for us to do. (*Ephesians 2:10*)

We hauled the old couch out the door last night. It's been demoted from the living room to the basement. The cushions we once carefully guarded by banning all food and drink from their presence will now be the dog's winter sleeping quarters. After all, it's just the basement couch. No one will care if red Kool-Aid spills across its pillows. No one will give a thought to the buttons on the back when they come loose. After a few years in the basement it will be demoted again, this time to the living room of some newlywed couple before making its final stop: the curb.

Carrying the old couch out the door brought back memories of when we carried it in. My wife and I were so excited back then, before the cushions were barraged by baby girl spit-up, toddler potty-training accidents, and the sodas I spilled while watching the Yankees. (I tend to get a little excited during Yankee games.) It was our first new piece of living room furniture, replacing the old parent-to-newlywed-hand-me-down my parents gave us. It went to the curb. Out with the old, in with the new.

Eleven years, four living rooms in four states, and four thousand miles in moving vans later, the new couch was old, one step away from the curb. The thought made me a little sad, not because I miss a sofa whose springs have lost all their spring, but because of the futility of it all. Furniture wears out. As do televisions. And microwave ovens. And cars. And clothes. All of the things to which Western man devotes his time and energy make the same journey from the showroom to the curb, with a few stops in between. Carrying my old couch out the door made me realize that we live in a culture where mankind's main purpose is to keep the trash collectors busy.

The thought made me depressed, until I turned to the promise of God: "For we are God's workmanship, created in Christ Jesus to do good works, which God prepared in advance for us to do" (Ephesians 2:10).

Long before we were born again, long before we were born, long before the physical universe was spoken into existence, God planned a life of purpose for you and me. His plan results in a finished product that will never be set by the curb, waiting for the trash truck to haul it away. Jesus promises that we can store up treasure in heaven by pursuing His kingdom. This promise applies to more than a select few individuals. God holds it out to everyone who is willing to embrace His Son.

God's purpose for our lives is "to do good works, which God prepared in advance for us to do." He started planning long ago for us to do more than help an occasional old lady across the street or other acts that might help us win a merit badge.

While most of us struggle to find more specific details, 1 Corinthians 6:19–20 gives us a simple formula for what He has in mind for us: "You are not your own; you were bought at a price. Therefore honor God with your body." Our purpose in this life is to use our bodies and all of our physical resources to honor God. These are the good works He created us to do.

Such simple instructions open up a world of opportunities. Anything and everything I do can be a part of the good works He prepared in advance for me to do, when I do it for the glory of God. Ultimately, God wants me to use my life to point people to Him. Your life and mine are to be like mirrors, reflecting God's glory to the people around us through our actions. As others see our good works, they won't praise us but our Father in heaven (Matthew 5:16). Ultimately, our lives should draw people to the Lord so that they can find God's purpose for their lives in Christ.

Looking across the street at the trash at the curb in front of my neighbor's house makes the whole idea of something better very appealing. That is, until I read the fine print. Actually the print isn't fine at all. I just don't like what it says; at least, not all the time. The fine print informs me that living according to the promise of God's purpose for my life cannot be a part-time pursuit. Jesus said, "If anyone would come after me, he must deny himself and take up his cross daily and follow me" (Luke 9:23). Every day I must make the same decision. Deny self, take up my cross, and follow Christ— every day for a lifetime. A lifetime! I cringe at the thought of surrendering *all* of my hopes and

dreams for my life to the will of God. That is, until I
seriously consider the options.

Every one of us has two options lying before
us. The sum total of everything our lives accomplish will end up in one of two places, the curb or
heaven. Without the promise of purpose there was
only one option. Everything would waste away, all
of our efforts would be for nothing. Now our Lord
has promised us something far greater. He promises
us a life of purpose. God's plan can be difficult to
pursue, and He does not force us to follow it. But I
do not want to stand at the end of my life and
watch my life's work being compacted in the back
of a trash truck. Praise God, He has other plans for
you and me.

25

HOPE

Praise be to the God and Father of our Lord Jesus Christ! In his great mercy he has given us new birth into a living hope through the resurrection of Jesus Christ from the dead, and into an inheritance that can never perish, spoil or fade—kept in heaven for you. (1 Peter 1:3–4)

They have a look. Words can hardly describe it. Once you see it you never forget it. It begins with their eyes—hollow, lifeless eyes. Eyes that would rather stay closed; eyes that see because nature forces them to receive light. If the eye is the window to the soul, these windows reveal a vast emptiness, like windows to a home gutted by fire, a fire that robbed a family of someone they loved. Sad doesn't quite describe them, nor does any other emotion. They are empty, lifeless.

The look descends down their faces like a shroud. You walk away thinking their complexions were pale. The color of death radiates from deep inside them. In a very real sense they are dead. Their lives are spent waiting for their bodies to join their souls in the grave.

Inside the prison walls they are the men without hope, those sentenced to die either at the hand of the state or by the hand of time.

Inmates without hope do not survive very long. When all hope for release is snatched away, when every avenue for appeal is removed, the captives begin to change into something more animal than human. The prisoners' shoulders reveal the look. Rolled forward, broken, like dogs beaten one too many times. They don't walk with confidence and defiance anymore. The big cats in the zoo have the same gait, an anxious pacing, shuffling back and forth. Waiting. Wondering. Watching. Helpless. Hopeless. Like the lions and tigers, these men also live in cages.

This same hopeless condition has descended upon the culture in which we live. We live among a people without hope, people who have bought the lie that this world is all there is, people who every day become a little less human. Pessimism reigns, and cynicism is the order of the day, for nothing really matters.

In the midst of this doom and gloom, God offers the promise of hope. Because Jesus rose from the dead, we have the hope, the absolute guarantee from God, that in Him we too will live forever. But eternal life is more than a continuation of our present existence. The centerpiece of our hope is the knowledge that one day soon we will be ushered into the presence of God where we will stay forever and ever. There is more than this life; death is not the end. All that we were created for lies before us in Christ.

But the hope we have in Christ does more than give us something to look forward to once this life is over. Hope compels us to leave our comfort zones and go out to the people and places where hopelessness abounds. In Matthew 25, Jesus describes the day when all of mankind will stand before Him to be judged. People will be divided into two groups, the sheep and the goats. The

sheep are those who staked their hope on Jesus; the
goats are those who rejected Him. The distinguish-
ing characteristic between the two is the things they
did or did not do. Those who follow Christ are
marked by their eagerness to feed the hungry, re-
fresh the thirsty, show hospitality to strangers,
clothe the naked, and visit those in prison. Read
over that list again. Those who have staked their
eternal destiny on Jesus will be known by rolling
up their sleeves and involving themselves in the
lives of those who hurt.

What I find remarkable is the reaction of these
people when Jesus commends them for their actions: "Then the righteous will answer him, 'Lord,
when did we see you hungry. . . ?'" (Matthew
25:37). Reading the passage I get the impression
that they are a bit embarrassed being singled out by
Jesus. During their lifetimes they never thought
what they were doing was remarkable or worthy of
praise. They simply did what had to be done. People with the hope of Christ naturally go to those
who are trapped in despair and act.

And there is a lot to do. The work never ends.
We feed the hungry, but thousands still die of star-
vation; we clothe the naked, yet poverty still runs
rampant; we visit prisoners, but crime keeps growing and growing. It is an endless cycle, as old as
mankind. We invade hopeless situations with the
hope of Christ, but we come away wondering if we
are wasting our time. Sins remain, and evil seems to
grow, especially in our modern world. Social ills
like abortion and crime seem to have stripped away
society's stability; indeed, no one feels comfortable
walking the streets at night. Prayer left the public

school nearly a generation ago and nothing has been able to bring it back.

The world gets worse; we have to ask if our presence makes any difference at all. Many of us throw up our hands in disgust and conclude that there is nothing for us to do but sing songs of heaven and wait for Jesus to come back.

Yet biblical hope doesn't disappoint; it encourages us to keep working (Romans 5:5). It doesn't try to rid the world of every problem and bring in a utopian world. Rather, hope invades those problems with the hope and love of Jesus Christ. We feed the hungry not because we believe that we will someday end all hunger but because God commands us to love the poor and care for them. We go into prisons not because we believe we can end the problem of crime but because God commands us to love the prisoner and to care for those the world has tried to throw away. Just as God has given us hope, we must give it away to the hopeless.

26

PROVISION

And my God will meet all your needs according to his glorious riches in Christ Jesus. *(Philippians 4:19)*

I think I live in the wrong place and the wrong time to fully understand what God promises to do when He says that He will meet all our needs according to His glorious riches in Christ Jesus. On the surface the promise looks straightforward. Have a need? Present it to the Lord and He will take care of it. Not just one or two, but all of them. No need to worry about His resources running short. His capacity to provide for you and me is measured in terms of the riches that are in Christ Jesus. Since He owns everything, God can do anything. And that is just what He promises to do.

I think He promises to do that . . . or maybe He doesn't. To be honest, I'm not so sure. I live in a time and place where the word *need* has been stretched beyond recognition. I don't have to go far to find examples. All I need to do is think back on my most recent day. In the last twenty-four hours I have boldly declared that I need everything from a two-liter bottle of carbonated beverage to a new car (actually, a less-old car). Every day is pretty much the same. From the time I get up in the morning to the time I go to bed, I constantly see things around the house that need to be replaced, or advertisements for gadgets I'm told I cannot live without.

Before you jump to the conclusion that I am some sort of spoiled brat, listen to the words that flow from your own lips. Judging by our conversation, we are the neediest people in all the world. Does God promise to meet all these needs, if you can call them needs? Do we really expect God to take care of this barrage of requests that we lay at His feet every day? I think we do. Not all these are needs, of course. I doubt if any of us drop to our knees and ask for a soda, but we do spend much of our prayer time asking for a world of other things that are just as unimportant. All the while we point back to the verse that opens this chapter as the promise upon which we pin our prayers, "My God shall supply all your needs according to his glorious riches in Christ Jesus."

Our other favorite provision passage is Psalm 37:25: "I was young and now I am old, yet I have never seen the righteous forsaken or their children begging bread." The latter is usually quoted whenever there is more month than paycheck.

Yet the Bible has many stories about the righteous who seem to have been forsaken. Jesus Himself told the story of a righteous man named Lazarus, a man who spent his days begging at a rich man's doorstep. Dogs ate better than Lazarus. The old beggar finally died from what appears to be malnutrition or another malady associated with extreme poverty. He begged for bread, yet he went to heaven when he died. How does the promise relate to poor old Lazarus?

Or to us?

When we take a serious look at all the Scripture passages relating to God's promise to provide for our physical needs, we find one common denominator. All focus on our need for something other than physical resources. In fact, physical needs such as food, clothing, and shelter are not even a secondary issue in the eyes of God. Jesus assured us that just as our Father cares for the birds and flowers He will care for us (Matthew 6:25–34). Instead of worrying about what we will eat or what we will wear, we must pursue the kingdom of God and His righteousness. When Paul assured the church in Philippi that God would meet all their needs, he was encouraging them to continue to give sacrificially, as they had already been doing.

Significantly, Psalm 37:26, which immediately follows the verse that states, "I have never seen the righteous forsaken or their children begging bread," says, "They [the righteous] are always generous and lend freely." Neither passage was meant to imply that God will shower us with every desire of our heart. Rather, both echo the words of Christ in the Sermon on the Mount, "But seek first his kingdom and his righteousness, and all these things will be given to you as well" (Matthew 6:33).

What then does God promise to provide? Peter tells us that God has given us everything we need for life and godliness, those things that will enable us to participate in the divine nature and escape the corruption in the world caused by evil desires (2 Peter 1:3–4). Nowhere in Scripture does He promise to provide us with a second car or a larger house or the money to pay the oral surgeon for pulling our wisdom teeth. He does promise to supply everything we need to fulfill His purpose for our lives.

Remember, before Paul wrote that God would supply all our needs, he also wrote, "I know what it is to be in need. . . . I have learned the secret of being content . . . whether well fed or hungry" (Philippians 4:12). Following Christ may well lead us to places where some of our favorite needs cannot and will not be satisfied. He hasn't stopped being faithful to us or to His Word.

Even in those moments where we must learn to be content with less than we desire, we will find God has provided us exactly what we need. In the midst of a culture that thinks we must have everything, perhaps our greatest need is to do without so that we might learn that the Lord is all we truly need.

27

FRUIT

> "I am the vine; you are the branches. If a man remains in me and I in him, he will bear much fruit; apart from me you can do nothing. . . . This is to my Father's glory, that you bear much fruit, showing yourselves to be my disciples." *(John 15:5, 8)*

I grew up in the suburbs and don't know much about agriculture. I don't know when you should plant corn or harvest soy beans. Flowers start out as seeds, but they all look pretty much the same to me when they come up. Pansy or petunia, who knows which is which? Flora and fauna might as well be small furry characters in an animated motion picture. The only way for me to get a green thumb is to dip my hand in lime Jell-O.

But even my horticulturally challenged mind knows how to tell the difference between trees. My family and I spent five years living next to a fifty-acre citrus grove. Like an expert I could walk out my door and automatically tell the difference between navel and Valencia orange trees and between lemon and grapefruit trees. Their leaves looked very similar; the trunks had the same gnarled look to them. But I could tell the difference. I simply waited until November when the fruit matured and changed colors. Orange trees always bear oranges, never lemons. Look for the fruit and you will discover what kind of tree is in your backyard.

Our lives are like trees; they constantly bear

fruit. Every day is harvest day for the trees of our lives. Something drops to the ground from our branches. People pick up our fruit, inspect it, and make decisions about what kind of tree we really are. No one really cares what we call ourselves. They rarely pay attention to the labels we hang around our necks or the bold statements we make about who we are and what we believe. Our fruit tells them all they need to know. It reveals more about ourselves than we want anyone to uncover. But we can't hide it. Those oranges laying around our trunks give us away.

A tree is known by its fruit. The reality of our walk with God is revealed by the fruit of our lives. We will produce a harvest of some kind. Galatians 5 surveys the options; there are really only two. One crop flows out of our sinful nature. It includes such delectable tidbits as sexual immorality, impurity, hatred, discord, jealousy, selfish ambition, dissension, envy, and drunkenness, just to name a few (Galatians 5:19–21). We don't need to do anything to make these drop from our branches. They all flow naturally from our lives when we live for ourselves.

The other crop Paul lists in Galatians is not natural, but supernatural. It is produced by the Spirit of God working within us. The fruit of the Spirit is love, joy, peace, patience, kindness, goodness, faithfulness, gentleness, and self-control (Galatians 5:22–23). Note that Paul did not list these as the *fruits* of the Spirit but as the *fruit,* the evidence of the Spirit's presence in our lives. As we "live by the Spirit" and "keep in step with the Spirit" (Galatians

5:25), He will make His presence known in an unmistakable way.

Just as you cannot find both oranges and lemons on the same tree, you will not find the fruit of the flesh and the fruit of the Spirit in the same life. Either the tree will be good and its fruit will be good, or the tree will be bad and the fruit will be bad. Trees are known by their fruit.

Trees in the backyard cannot change themselves, but the tree of each of our lives can be transformed. It can bear fruit for God. In fact, the Lord promises to make our lives fruitful for Him. Yet it is a conditional promise. Our harvest will not change automatically without action on our part. We must stop being our own tree—bearing the fruit of the flesh—and become a branch grafted into the Lord Jesus Christ—bearing the fruit of the Spirit. Jesus Himself said, "I am the vine; you are the branches. If a man remains in me and I in him, he will bear much fruit; apart from me you can do nothing" (John 15:5). The Bible calls such "grafting in" *repentance*. We must realize that the sin in our lives comes from deep within ourselves, from our own fallen nature. The problem is not the soil over our roots or the other trees in the grove. Repentance confesses that the fruit of our lives is bad because we are fundamentally flawed; we need to be transformed.

This transformation comes as we cling to Christ by faith. Paul wrote, "For it is by grace you have been saved, through faith" (Ephesians 2:8). Faith means believing that Jesus is the Son of God who came and died in our place and rose again the third day. But it does not stop at merely accepting this as a historical fact. To believe in Him means to place our lives in His hands, to follow Him throughout our lives. When we place our faith in Him, He pulls up our old tree and grafts us into Himself, like a branch in a vine.

After we are grafted into Christ, we must remain in Him and He in us. Jesus said, "I am the vine; you are the branches. If a man remains in me and I in him, he will bear much fruit; apart from me you can do nothing" (John 15:5; see also 15:6–8). This word picture describes an intimate relationship between our Savior and us. To remain in Him means to cling to Him and to know Him more every day. This also speaks of our utter dependence upon Him. As John 15 points out, this dynamic comes about as God's Word dwells within us and we respond through prayer.

Just as a branch depends completely upon the vine to produce fruit through it, we must depend upon the Lord to produce His fruit through us. Love, joy, peace, and all the other fruit of righteousness don't spring up from our human efforts. They come as a direct result of the inner working of the Holy Spirit of God. Remember, they are the fruit of the Spirit, not the fruit of a Christian. When the Spirit strengthens His hold upon our lives, we bear fruit for God.

The question is not whether we will bear fruit. The question is, What kind of fruit will we bear? God promises to make our lives fruitful for Him, if we are willing to do what it takes to make the promise a reality.

28

UNDERSTANDING

"For who has known the mind of the Lord that he may instruct him?" But we have the mind of Christ. *(1 Corinthians 2:16)*

A huge gulf separates the human race from God. Sin makes the chasm wider, but it is made up of more than sin. God is so unlike us that our minds cannot grasp who He is or what He is like. We struggle with time; He lives in eternity. We are finite; He is infinite. Our universe consists of that which we can see and experience; He knows no such limits. We are weak; His power is unlimited. And finally, we are sinful, whereas He is holy.

In many ways we are like fish swimming in an aquarium. All we know, all that we see, is inside a ten-gallon tank. Our entire frame of reference consists of water, rocks, a plastic diving guy with bubbles coming out of his head, and artificial plants. The tank doesn't seem small because we've never experienced anything else. A few of the others in the tank talk about a bigger body of water that lies beyond the glass walls, but such talk sounds foolish. The aquarium is all there is and all there ever will be. It's all we have ever known.

God is to us what we are to a fish, with one crucial difference. Fish in an aquarium can never understand life beyond the tank. Their feeble little

minds are much too small. But God made us in His
image in order that we might know Him and have a
dynamic relationship with Him. Though sin dark-
ens our understanding to the point that we even
doubt His existence, God in His mercy opens our
eyes to His truth. He gives us the promise of understanding.

The promise of understanding changes our
lives long before we claim it as our own. In our natural state, in the fish tank, our minds are blinded.
We "cannot see the light of the gospel of the glory
of Christ" (2 Corinthians 4:4). The futility of our
thinking traps us, our hearts become hardened by
sin, which leaves us stuck in ignorance. Left to ourselves we would die in this state. No one ever turns
to Christ on his own. But God reaches down and opens our eyes, giving us "the light of the knowledge
of the glory of God in the face of Christ" (2 Corinthians 4:6). As a result we understand that Jesus is
the Christ, the Son of the living God, and rise to
new lives in Him (Matthew 16:16).

After our eyes are opened by the gospel of
Christ, we are never again trapped in a fish-tank
perspective. God begins planting His thoughts inside of us through His Holy Spirit, giving us real
wisdom and understanding. Paul summed up this
process by declaring, "we have the mind of Christ"
(1 Corinthians 2:16). Hold on tight because this is
where the promise really gets exciting. The mind of
Christ allows us to understand the things of God.
All of those sermons and songs and Bible stories
that seemed like so much mumbo jumbo suddenly
begin to make sense. The Holy Spirit takes us by

the hand and opens our heart to all that God has freely given us (see 1 Corinthians 2:12).

God also gives us a fresh perspective on the world around us. We see that there really is more to life than the water and rocks and the plastic diving guy. The promise of understanding lets us see how temporary, and therefore insignificant, these things are. Houses and cars and all the other things that seemed so important before we met Christ are nothing in comparison to knowing Him. And the wisdom of the world no longer sounds quite as wise. Those who say that the fish tank is all there is and all there ever will be no longer sound profound but foolish.

The promise of understanding revolves around the greatest expression of God to man, the Bible. No longer is it a closed book to us; now we read its pages and can hear the voice of God speak directly to us. We see ourselves in the stories, we hear His commands echo through the letters. Because God freely gives the promise of understanding to everyone who follows His Son by faith, every believer has the capability to read and understand the Word of God.

Like most of God's gifts, the promise of understanding comes with a set of responsibilities. First, we must use this new understanding to the best of our abilities. God never drops a load of knowledge from heaven into our brains. By His Spirit He has opened our hearts and minds so that we can understand (2 Corinthians 4:4, 6). Now we must study His Word, meditate upon it, and apply it to our lives. The promise of understanding also needs to be applied to all our endeavors in life. When it is unleashed, it will change the way we see the world around us and the way in which we respond to it.

Ultimately, God gives us understanding in order that we might walk in obedience to Him. The psalmist cried out, "Give me understanding, and I will keep your law and obey it with all my heart" (Psalm 119:34). Unless understanding is translated into obedience, we are nothing more than the smartest fish in the aquarium, still trapped by its glass walls.

Our Lord is not concerned with expanding our minds, but with changing our lives. The more we know, the more we understand, the more we will strive to be like Christ.

29

BLESSING

Praise be to the God and Father of our Lord Jesus Christ, who has blessed us in the heavenly realms with every spiritual blessing in Christ. *(Ephesians 1:3)*

God bless America.
And bless this food to the nourishment of our bodies.
And bless Mom and Dad.
And bless Your church.
And the missionaries.
Bless this house.
Bless this car.
Bless the guy who sneezed.
Bless this mess.

Bless me.
Especially, bless me.
And this project I am trying to finish.
And the home I am struggling to build.
And the children I am doing my best to raise.
And me.
Don't forget about me.
Bless me.

I know You are in the business of blessing people.
You blessed Adam and Eve.
And Noah.
And Abraham. And Isaac. And Jacob.

You blessed Joseph.
And Moses.
And the people of Israel.
And me?

Maybe I should start.
Maybe I should start by blessing You.
I bless You, O Lord.
What does that mean?
When I hope that You will bless me, I'm not
    really asking for houses or land or stuff.
That stuff always seems to come between You
    and me.
Too much stuff, not enough You.

I bless You, O Lord.
I guess I mean thank You.
Thank You for everything.
Thank You for my wife.
Thank You for my family.
Thank You for my stuff.
Most of all, thank You for You.
For Your Son.
For Your Spirit.
For You.

If I did not have a wife, thank You for You.
If I did not have a family, thank You for You.
If I did not have any stuff, thank You for You.
If I had nothing at all, thank You for You.
For You are the blessing I desire.
And You have given me so much.

Your blessings are so numerous I can hardly
    count them.
It starts with the way You chose me to be holy
    and blameless in Your sight.
And then You adopted me into Your family;
    I never expected that one.
And You redeemed me.
And You forgave me.
And showed me your mysteries.
And placed me in Christ.
And sent Your Spirit to dwell within me.
And gave me an eternal inheritance.
You blessed me and I am blessed.

I thank You.
I will worship You.
I will obey You.
I will follow You.
May my life be a blessing to others,
Because You have blessed me.
And I bless You, O Lord.
I love You.

30

SATISFACTION

> Jesus answered, "Everyone who drinks
> this water will be thirsty again, but whoever
> drinks the water I give him will never thirst.
> Indeed, the water I give him will become in
> him a spring of water welling up to eternal
> life." (*John 4:13–14*)

Carefully read the above passage. Concentrate
on the phrase, "Whoever drinks the water I
give him will never thirst." Jesus Himself spoke
these words to a Samaritan woman alongside a well
near the city of Sychar. She thought He was talking
about physical water, an offer she was eager to accept. Every day she had to walk to the well with an
empty pot, fill it, and lug the heavy jar back to her
home. Anything that could relieve her of this duty
sounded good to her. But Jesus was not talking
about H$_2$O.

The water Jesus offered was a spring of spiritual water that wells up to eternal life in those who
drink it. Jesus offered relief for her—and our—
greatest need, a thirst too deep to describe with
words.

As you again read the opening passage, let the
words of Jesus sink in as if you had never heard
them before. Now let me ask you a question. Do
you believe that Jesus can and will satisfy your
deepest thirst? Do you believe His words to the
woman at the well?

Most of us say we do indeed believe Jesus'

words. He satisfies the longing of our souls. Without Him we wander, looking for some mysterious something. What that "something" may be we do not know. We're not even sure if it can be found. But once we find Him our search is over. He is all we need.

With Him we are truly satisfied.

Or are we?

Are you? Am I? Just thinking about the words I am about to pen makes me very uneasy. They force me to be totally honest with God, and being honest with God can be a very dangerous thing. I am not so sure that my actions tell the world that I am satisfied with Jesus—that what I've found satisfies my every longing.

Before you look down your nose at me, be sure to drop your mask. Be completely honest with yourself and with God. How satisfied are you really? I see so many people running from one spiritual experience to another, always looking for something new, always in search of something life changing, that I question how satisfied with Jesus any of us are. People change churches with the greatest of ease, all in search of that elusive congregation that will meet their needs. Americans shop for churches like we shop for cars. We want the latest accessories, the newest programs, the best music, making the search for a place of worship little more than sanctified consumerism.

I wonder sometimes how satisfied we are with Jesus when we use the words *want* and *need* so often. We want new clothes and new cars and new houses and new spouses. The old ones are too out of style with too many miles and too many faults.

That is different, you say. Wanting a new pair of shoes has very little to do with a spring of water that wells up to eternal life. But does it? Jesus once had another thirsty person come up to Him requesting the water of life. This man had everything he could possibly desire: houses, wealth, education, a prominent position in the community. The one thing he did not have was real satisfaction. His soul ached for something more out of life. "Teacher," he said to Jesus, "what good thing must I do to get eternal life?" (Matthew 19:16). Jesus told him to give everything he had to the poor and follow Him.

Jesus wasn't implying that poverty is the path to salvation. Rather, His words to the rich young man were very much like His words to the woman at the well. Once someone comes to know Him, he will not want anything else. Those who come to Christ will be perfectly satisfied with Him alone.

Most of us bear a strong semblance to Solomon in the book of Ecclesiastes. He tried parties and success and wealth and anything else he could think of in an attempt to run the meaninglessness out of his life. But nothing worked. As he surveyed all his hands had done, he found it all to be meaningless, pointless, like chasing after the wind (see Ecclesiastes 2:10–11). We have gadgets and gizmos and all sorts of conveniences that would make Solomon drool in envy, but we are no more satisfied than he was. Compared to the rest of the world we are incredibly wealthy and religious, yet we want more.

As Solomon dug a little deeper, he discovered the reason why life is so disappointing. Ecclesiastes 2:25 asks the question, "Without him, who can eat or find enjoyment?" God has made us in such a way that we cannot and will not ever find satisfaction in anything apart from Him. This does not mean that we need to add God to all our pursuits in order to find happiness. Rather, He must become the object of all our pursuits. Then and only then will we find that He truly does satisfy our deepest desires.

Perhaps I sound as though I am rambling. This chapter is less about writing and more about confessing. I confess that I continually battle with wanting more out of life. I wrestle with the desire to achieve success. I wrestle with the desire that the shine of a new car brings out in me. I wrestle with wanting more out of this life even though I know nothing this world has to offer can satisfy. I wrestle because I do not want to do what must be done to lay hold of the satisfaction God promises in His Son.

Jesus told the rich young ruler to leave everything behind to follow Him. His words apply to you and me as well. Only when we are willing to lose everything will we find the one thing we long for. When we lose our lives to Christ, we are satisfied. When we don't, we are not and cannot be. His promise is real. By faith we must let go of everything else in order to grasp Him alone. Only then will we find that He is all we want and need. He will satisfy.

Part 4

PROMISES THAT CARRY US THROUGH THE HARSHNESS OF LIFE

31

TRIALS

> Consider it pure joy, my brothers, whenever you face trials of many kinds. *(James 1:2)*

"Consider it pure joy whenever you face trials of many kinds." Wait . . . Stop the presses! Call in the editors, check the original manuscript. This has to be a misprint. Surely the apostle James meant to say that we should consider it pure joy whenever we *escape* trials of many kinds.

Yeah, that's probably what he had in mind. Escaping trials, that brings me joy, like the day the antilock brakes on my wife's car worked to perfection and she missed the car that pulled out in front of her. Trial escaped, and we were all pretty happy about it.

Or maybe James forgot to put the words *do not* in there somewhere. "Consider it pure joy whenever you *do not* face trials of many kinds," another way of saying rejoice when life is good. I like that version better. Count your blessings. Enjoy the good life, the trouble-free life. Smile, be happy, life is good. That makes more sense to our modern ears. Why, if James 1:2 is correct as printed, then that means we should be happy when our faith is put to the test. And if that is true, then that also means that God promises . . . trials?

Trials as a promise? We might as well ask for lumps of coal in our Christmas stockings or liver for a birthday dinner. Promises are supposed to be about things that are good for us, things we need to make it through life, stuff that will make us more like Christ. Give me some good old peace and joy and happiness and love. But trials?

It's not a misprint; James was not misquoted. God does not promise to give us a trouble-free life. In fact the very opposite is the case. Jesus encouraged His disciples and us with these words, "In this world you will have trouble" (John 16:33). You *will have* trouble, He said. Count on it. One of the men who heard these words firsthand later wrote, "Dear friends, do not be surprised at the painful trial you are suffering, as though something strange were happening to you" (1 Peter 4:12).

Before we file a protest with heaven, we need to remember that God is not the author of all our trials. James reminds us that we will face a wide variety of trials from different sources. There are times that God Himself puts our faith to the test. Abraham and Isaac had their faith in a good and loving God pushed to the limit when God instructed Abraham to offer Isaac as a burnt offering. In the end the Lord's hand stopped the sacrifice before Isaac's life could be taken, but only after Abraham's absolute trust in God and his willingness to obey had been proven genuine. Obedience to the Lord's command often throws us into situations we cannot control, situations we would have rather avoided, situations that force us to trust God like we never have before.

But many, if not most, of the trials we face do

not come directly from the hand of God. Some come as a natural result of the opposition a sinful world throws against those who desire to live for Christ. Paul reminded Timothy that everyone who desires to live a godly life will suffer for it (2 Timothy 3:12). Trials also take the form of temptation. Nothing puts our faith to the test quite like the lure of the forbidden. Wrestling with temptation while saying no to sin can be the most difficult trial we will ever face. Other trials come because of the presence of sin in the world. Death and disease and all the other things that make life on planet Earth unbearable are with us because sin now reigns. Coming down with the flu does not mean God is judging us for failing to tithe consistently. Rather, sickness entered the world with sin, and sickness will remain a part of our lives until Christ returns.

The above may imply that trials always take the form of negative circumstances, but that simply is not the case. The term translated *trial* in James 1:2 denotes any kind of test our faith endures, both positive and negative. For those who strive to follow Christ, prosperity can test our faith as much as adversity, success as much as failure. During hard times our faith is put on the line: Will we trust in God alone when we have nowhere else to turn? During good times the test is the same: Will we trust in God and honor Him when we have so many other options?

Whatever form they may take, in the hand of God trials serve a dual purpose. First, they test the validity of our faith. Jesus told the story of a farmer who walked along, slinging seeds in a field. Most of the seeds germinated, but not all of the plants sur-

vived. Some of the seeds fell into shallow, rocky soil.
The warmth of the soil caused the seeds to sprout
almost immediately, but the same sun that warmed
the soil soon scorched the plants, and they withered
away. The story of the farmer is the story of how the
good news of the kingdom touches people's hearts.
Many people receive the good news with great joy.
They want what Christ has to offer, especially when
their lives are not turning out the way they expected. Yet, trials come and show that their "faith" was
little more than a passing fancy. As Jesus explained,
the one who received the seed that fell on the rocky
places has temporary joy but no roots, and "when
trouble or persecution comes because of the word,
he quickly falls away" (Matthew 13:20–21).

Trials not only prove the validity of our faith,
they also purify our lives; suffering and trials break
the hold of sin over us. "He who has suffered in his
body is done with sin. As a result, he does not live
the rest of his earthly life for evil human desires, but
rather for the will of God" (1 Peter 4:1–2). Earlier in
the same book Peter compared the fire of trials with
the refining fire used to burn away impurities from
gold. In the eyes of God our faith is worth much
more than something as temporary as precious met-
als. Therefore God allows the heat and pain of trials
to burn away the impurities from our lives.

As we go on through this final section we will
explore the many forms trials take. From suffering
to persecution, trials will come. We will also explore the specific ways God demonstrates His
power through the worst the world can dish out.
No matter what we may face, God uses everything
for His eternal purpose.

32

CHRISTLIKENESS

Consider it pure joy, my brothers, whenever you face trials of many kinds, because
you know the testing of your faith develops
perseverance. Perseverance must finish its
work so that you may be mature and complete, not lacking anything. *(James 1:2–4)*

God has a goal for your life and mine, a goal so
big and so glorious that He is willing to do
whatever it takes to accomplish it. James speaks of
it in the key verses above; Paul expands on the idea
in Ephesians. James calls the goal *maturity;* Paul de-
fines maturity as "attaining to the whole measure of
the fullness of Christ" (Ephesians 4:13); that is, *to
be like Christ.* God plans to remake you and me in
the image of His Son. The end result will be that we
become totally new creatures, "created to be like
God in true righteousness and holiness" (Ephesians
4:24).

This is God's goal for your life and mine, and
He will go to whatever lengths necessary to make it
a reality. Whatever it takes. Time has proven that
nothing works as well as trials. In the previous
chapter we came face-to-face with the fact that our
faith will be tested on a regular basis. James 1:2
filled us in on this little surprise. As we read on in
James 1 we learn why God allows trials to come our
way and how we can consider them to be pure joy.
Through trials, God is moving us from immaturity
to maturity. The rough edges of our lives are being

lopped off while our character is polished to reflect Christ. A faith that is never tested is a faith that never grows. Tests and trials are always the entrance exams to the next level of spiritual maturity.

God is willing to do whatever it takes because the end result is so valuable. He longs to see the character of Christ duplicated within us. Righteousness and holiness top the list of traits God wants to produce in us. We've wasted enough time on sin; our lives need to reflect the perfect light of the holiness of God. Righteousness and holiness go far beyond simply saying no to sin. To be holy means to be set apart for God's use; to be righteous means to allow God's righteousness to flow through us into the world. Fleeing from temptation is only part of the equation. Our Lord longs to see us pursue justice and mercy.

"Attaining to the whole measure of the fullness of Christ" also means Jesus' passion will become our passion. He was driven by the desire to do the will of the Father. Over and over Jesus reminded His listeners that He came to do the will of the One who sent Him (see John 4:34). Becoming mature in Christ brings an ever-increasing desire to lose our will to the will of God. Self-willed people may show up at church every Sunday, and they may even succeed in avoiding most of the world's vices; but they hardly reflect the character of Jesus. Only those who deny themselves, take up their cross daily, and follow Christ are drawing near to God's goal for their lives.

The heart of God's will is for every believer to become a servant. Jesus Himself declared that He did not come to be served but to serve. In case any of us were a little confused about what He meant, He washed His disciples' feet on His final night on earth. "I have set you an example that you should do as I have done for you" (John 13:15), Jesus told the Twelve when He was finished. This same example stands for us. Jesus came to give His life away. As the Father works to make us more like the Son, He will constantly and consistently break our pride and make us servants.

No one will ever stoop to serve another with his pride intact. God knows this. Therefore, He sets out to humble us. He isn't being mean-spirited, nor does He take any joy out of watching us fall on our faces. Yet God's goal for our lives is much too important to be laid on the altar of our egos. To be Christlike is to be humble. Since God promises to do everything necessary to remake us in the image of His Son, He will also humble us when our pride threatens the work He has planned for our lives.

Not the least of the qualities God wants to implant in us is His love. John 13:35 tells us that the mark of a Christian is love. The biblical term for love goes far beyond feelings to describe an act of dying to self and placing another person before ourselves. Love always expresses itself in action just as God demonstrated His love to us by giving His only Son. He longs to reproduce this same sacrificial love within each of us.

All of the above is not some religious ideal. Like the rest of the promises of God, we can count on the fact that He will bring this to pass. But He doesn't drop a transformed character on us in our sleep. Christlike character qualities are developed over time through the fires of trials. James described this as a process God takes each of us through. Trials produce perseverance, and perseverance develops maturity.

Perseverance is the step between the excitement that marks the early stages of our walk with God and the maturity He longs to produce in us. When trials strike, many who started on the journey turn back. They suddenly realize that this God and Jesus business isn't what they bargained for. But those who have truly been born again will persevere. As they do, their perseverance grows into Christlike character.

Paul describes this same process in Romans 5:3–4: "We also rejoice in our sufferings, because we know that suffering produces perseverance; perseverance, character; and character, hope." The path to character comes through the hard road of persevering under trial.

I often wonder why the process has to be like this. Why does the road have to be so difficult? Looking back on my own life I realize that there could be no other way. When life is easy I never have to grow. My faith is never forced to climb to a higher level. I don't want to limp along with a childish faith. I long to see God's goal come to pass in my life. Whatever it takes.

33

SUFFERING

For it has been granted to you on behalf
of Christ not only to believe on him, but also
to suffer for him. (*Philippians 1:29*)

Suffering. As I write that word, the faces of people
flash through my mind. I think of a friend in
California who lost her fight with cancer, leaving
behind a husband and two young children. I see
the face of a mother staring back at me from the
front row in a funeral home as she buries her thir-
teen-year-old son. More images come at me. People
who suffer with chronic illness, people who have
lost everything because of a lost job, people whose
children rebel against them and God.

These are ordinary people. Yet they form a select group—people who have known suffering
firsthand. I cannot shake the images. They haunt
me as I try to write what must be said: Suffering is a
gift granted by God.

I can write "Suffering is a gift" while sitting in
the cozy comfort of my study, but I don't think I
could bring myself to say the words out loud. Not
even when I am alone. The sound of them frightens
me. Maybe *frighten* isn't the right word. The sound
of the words shakes me. It reminds me how thin
the veil is between those who suffer and those of us
who do not. But the most haunting thought of all is

that I may be on the wrong side of the veil. Visiting a hospital room is much easier than residing in it, but that doesn't mean I am more blessed. In fact, the very opposite may be true—for with suffering comes distinct blessing.

But could I bring myself to share that thought with people sitting in a surgery waiting area? I never have. The opportunity presents itself time and time again, but my mind will never issue the command to my mouth. Silence replaces the promise. Paul told the church in Philippi that suffering had been granted to them by the grace of God. The word Paul uses describes the giving of a gift or the bestowal of a huge privilege upon someone. Look up, he told them; stand firm. God hasn't forgotten you. On the contrary. He has given you a wonderful gift, the gift of suffering.

In a sense, I can explain away Paul's words and justify my silence. The suffering the church in Philippi endured came as a result of their stand for Christ. They suffered for the sake of righteousness. Such suffering is closer to persecution, a subject we will explore in detail in a later chapter. Christians in the Arab world encounter persecution every day. In Iran, spreading the gospel of Jesus Christ is punishable by death. The men and women who take a stand for Christ there share in the privilege given to the church in Philippi. They are suffering for the gospel.

To those of us who have never endured such suffering, we see this as more palatable or easier to understand. There is a definite group of bad guys, Islamic extremists, who are persecuting the good guys, our brothers and sisters in Christ. Believers are suffering because of evil in the world. We know that the persecutors ultimately will be repaid in full for what they have done. The Lord will not leave unpunished those who take the lives of those He loves.

But suffering for the cause of Christ is not the only suffering God grants us. We also suffer so that we can witness the power of God in us. In 2 Corinthians 11 Paul boasted of his sufferings for this reason. Some of his experiences are what we would expect. He was stoned by an angry mob because he dared to preach the gospel; he spent many a night in prison for the same reason. However, much of the suffering he endured did not come at the hands of angry men. Paul described being shipwrecked, being in danger from rivers, suffering from sleep deprivation and hunger. In addition, he wrestled with "a thorn in my flesh" (2 Corinthians 12:7), some sort of deep ailment that caused Paul incessant suffering. Any and all of these could have easily been prevented by a simple act of God. Yet He did not prevent them, and Paul counted them all as a privilege.

This is where all this talk of suffering becomes very uncomfortable. When the Scripture says that suffering has been granted to us by the hand of God, it does not mean that God Himself is personally afflicting us. Nor does it mean that we are to embrace suffering for suffering's sake, as if it were a good thing. Rather, we are to see suffering as an instrument God uses to bestow blessings on us we could never receive any other way. The greatest of these blessings is that of fellowship with the Lord Himself (Philippians 3:10). There is a depth of fellowship with God that can only be experienced through the pain of suffering.

In my first book, *Uncommon Adventures,* I told the story of Ruth Smith, a godly woman whose life was cut short by lung cancer. I will never forget how she spoke of her cancer as a blessing because of the intimacy with the Lord she experienced through it. In times of trouble, when our world crashes down around us, we find that our Lord is closer than He has ever been before. Words cannot describe the fellowship He grants in that moment, although we catch a glimpse of it in the story of Stephen's death as recorded in Acts 7.

Suffering also bestows other privileges. It enables us to know the Lord's resurrection power. It confirms our faith to a skeptical world and loudly proclaims the gospel. More than anything, suffering in this world whets our appetite for the world to come. No one who daily battles the pain of arthritis wants to spend any more time on planet Earth than is absolutely necessary. Instead, the pains in their joints remind them of the glory that awaits at the end of the journey.

I still see the faces. I still see the hurt in their eyes. I know that there will come a day when I will join their ranks. All of us will encounter suffering. As we do we will also find that the good promises God makes regarding suffering are really true.

34

PROTECTION

The angel of the Lord encamps around those who fear him, and he delivers them. (*Psalm 34:7*)

In light of the last few chapters, the above verse may sound hollow. On the one hand we talk about trials as an absolute certainty: In this life we will face trouble; trials of many kinds strike us when we least expect it. But the psalmist tells us that God promises to encamp around us, protect us, and rescue us from adversity. In this world we will experience pain and heartache and suffering. Yet over it all sits the Angel of the Lord, protecting us and rescuing us, all the days of our lives. How can both of these ideas be in the Bible?

Not only are the promises of trials and protection both in the Bible, but they frequently stand side by side. Jacob was a man whose life was marked by difficulties. Consider these calamaties: His schemes against his brother forced him to flee for his life; his father-in-law deceived him and forced twenty years of labor out of him; the one true love of his life died in childbirth; and his only daughter was raped. Add to that ten of his sons turning on his favorite son, selling him into slavery; they covered their crime by telling Jacob that his beloved Joseph was dead. The picture of his life that unfolds in the book of Genesis reveals one trial after another, heartache building on heartache. Yet at the end of his life Jacob called God "the Angel who has delivered me from all harm" (Genesis 48:16).

Nearly two thousand years later Peter wrote to a group of struggling Christians, encouraging them that they were "through faith . . . shielded by God's power until the coming . . . salvation" (1 Peter 1:5). The word translated "shielded" means to build a protective wall complete with guard towers and soldiers on patrol, like the giant walls that surrounded cities in the ancient Near East. A walled city was a safe haven whose residents could sleep securely at night. Believers in Christ are surrounded by the wall of the power of Almighty God. Yet Peter's very next sentence (verse 6) says, "Though now for a little while you may have had to suffer grief in all kinds of trials." God's power protects us, yet we now suffer grief in all kinds of trials.

Even Psalm 34:7, the verse that posed this quandary to us at the beginning of the chapter, combines the dual ideas of God's protection and present suffering. The verse was written by David, a man after God's own heart (Acts 13:22). We know him best as the man who killed the giant Goliath and as the greatest king in Israel's history. But when he wrote these words, the prospect of becoming king seemed like a cruel joke. His mighty exploits in battle had been turned against him by the reigning king, Saul. Accusing David of treason against the throne, Saul and all of Israel's armies hunted the future king like a dog. David penned the words of the thirty-fourth psalm while fleeing for his life.

He was alone, abandoned, forgotten. The only

place David could find to hide was in one of the cities of Israel's archenemies, the Philistines. Even there he had to pretend to be insane to keep from being killed. It was during this period of David's life that he wrote, "The angel of the Lord encamps around those who fear him, and he delivers them."

Obviously, we can conclude that God's protection does not exempt us from trouble, but that does not cast doubt on God's power. The book of Job begins in the throne room of heaven. There God reigns and all of the angels, both heavenly and fallen, come and present themselves before Him. In this scene Satan comes to receive permission to test the one man who shines out as faithful above all others, Job. Even after he is granted permission to begin the trials, Satan finds his power strictly limited by God. In Job we see firsthand the promise of 1 Corinthians 10:13, "God is faithful; he will not let you be tempted [tested] beyond what you can bear."

God Himself does stand guard over us. Psalm 91:10 calls us to make the Most High our refuge; "Then no harm will befall you, no disaster will come near your tent. For he will command his angels concerning you to guard you in all your ways." Trials, hardship, pain, disease, the loss of a job, and a host of other things that we lie awake at night dreading may well strike us—but they never take God by surprise. Nothing can ever secretly climb over the wall He builds around our lives. Nor can anything attack us that will thwart God's plan for our lives. No matter what we may face, God is in control.

The protection of God also reassures us that He

will never leave us to face adversity alone. "Never will I leave you; never will I forsake you," He promises in Hebrews 13:5. Therefore, we can say, "The Lord is my helper; I will not be afraid" (verse 6).

Shadrach, Meshach, and Abednego knew what it meant to suffer and yet have God's mighty protection. Uprooted from their childhood home by a conquering army, they were carried off to Babylon as slaves. The Babylonians soon recognized that they were no ordinary men and moved them into positions of responsibility. The meager comfort their positions gave was swept away the day Nebuchadnezzar declared himself to be a god and built a giant golden statue of himself. When Shadrach, Meshach, and Abednego refused to worship his image they were arrested and thrown into a fiery furnace. In the fire they found the angel of the Lord standing next to them, protecting them. He did not protect them from being cast into the fire, but He carried them through it.

God's promise to protect us still stands. His angels do stand guard over us. His power protects us. His Spirit stands beside us no matter what we may face. When the storms pass (and they always pass), we too will be able to see God's loving hand of mercy, carrying us along, protecting us from being destroyed. As a result, the adversity that threatens to shipwreck our faith only makes it stronger.

35

PERSECUTION

> But before all this, they will lay hands on you and persecute you. You will be betrayed by parents, brothers, relatives and friends, and they will put some of you to death. All men will hate you because of me. But not a hair of your head will perish. By standing firm you will save yourselves. (*Luke 21:12, 16–19*)

We live in a bubble in history and geography. We live in a time and place unlike much of the past two thousand years of church history. No one arrests Americans because of their faith. Indeed, in the Western world, few have to live in fear of death because they name the name of Christ. Americans as well as Canadians and Britons live in a bubble. A bubble of safety from persecution. A bubble of religious freedom. But a bubble can pop at any time.

Bubbles don't last long, for they are not the normal state of matters. At times we shout that our bubble has already burst. A politician or two will begin to talk about revoking the tax-exempt status of churches or applying strict zoning laws to our buildings and we confuse such opposition with outright persecution. "Woe is me," American Christians cry out, "the church is under attack." As we hear stories from other parts of the globe, however, we realize that our bubble is still intact. We are still safe, still inside the bubble.

I say we live in a bubble, for this brief respite from persecution is not the world of the past nor

the world as it shall be. Jesus told us how things
would be for His followers. "All men will hate you
because of me" (Luke 21:17). Strong words, words
that Jesus knew would be applied to Himself in a
matter of days. Less than a week after saying these
things to His disciples, Jesus was crucified. The
cheers of adulation degenerated into shouts of rage
and hatred. After Jesus died, the ever-growing
group of disciples incurred the wrath of their fellow
man. The book of Acts is filled with stories of
Christians being arrested, beaten, and killed. All
men hated them because of Christ. Most of the opposition the early church faced came not at the
hands of the Roman government but from their
neighbors and countrymen. An angry mob stoned
the apostle Paul outside the city of Iconium, an act
the Roman authorities would have surely stopped if
they had been present.

As the first century closed, the persecution of
the church grew more severe. The Roman government finally joined in, with empire-wide campaigns
against Christians. Entire families were tortured
and put to death. Those who were spared death lost
all their material goods. Christianity was not yet a
suburban, middle-class religion. People with property shied away from the outcasts. Remnants of
Roman graffiti include pictures mocking the core of
Christian beliefs.

With the passing of time successive waves of
persecution pounded against the church. At times
the governing authorities were responsible; other
shameful periods of history witnessed one "Christian" group trying to destroy another. Such acts of
violence sweep across the labels of Protestant and

Catholic; both groups are guilty. All the while those who sought to follow Christ found that all men hated them on account of His name.

Our own time has seen its share of persecution. Some experts estimate that more believers have died for the faith in the twentieth century than in the previous nineteen combined. From Chinese prisons to the Arab world to the mountains of Peru, followers of Christ in other parts of the world have lost everything, even their very lives, because of the gospel.

For the most part, however, those of us who live in North America experience persecution only through reading about it in books and magazines. Our bubble protects us. I must admit that I am glad that it does. But I have to wonder how different the religious face of America would be if the bubble were to burst. Our minds immediately assume the worst. The loss of religious freedom would be horrible; outlawing Christianity, unthinkable. Who would come to church if the authorities could crash through the doors at any time, hauling everyone in attendance off to jail? If we were ostracized by our family, excluded from every avenue of opportunity, forced to live at the very bottom of the social scale, who would want to be a part of us? How horrible it would be if we could not openly share our faith. What would we do? How could we win the world for Christ?

Why, if living for Jesus were against the law, if we were hated by everyone on account of Him, only those who really believed would dare associate with us. Only those who were absolutely convinced that Jesus is the way, the truth, and the life would dare wear the name of Christian. If evangelism could possibly land us in jail, everyone would remain silent except for those who were convinced that Jesus is the only hope. If that happened, the church in the United States would have a completely different look. It would look a lot like the first century church that changed an empire, instead of the anemic body that the world easily ignores today. That is the power of the promise of persecution. Persecution will make us stronger believers. In contrast, our present bubble has made us weaker and less effective for Christ.

The thing about bubbles is how easily they can pop. Some of you may have already experienced this. People in your neighborhood lash out at you with all sorts of cruel acts because of your stand for Christ. Coworkers ridicule you and do everything they can to try to make you fall, all because you will not compromise your convictions. Others of you may have been cut off from your family, virtually disowned because you shamed the family name by turning to Christ. You stand in good company, the company of history, the company of the apostles, the company of the Lord Himself.

"All men will hate you because of me. But not a hair of your head will perish. By standing firm you will save yourselves."

36

DELIVERANCE

> If this is so, then the Lord knows how to rescue godly men from trials and to hold the unrighteous for the day of judgment. *(2 Peter 2:9)*

Everyone else stayed in the boat. All twelve men saw the same phantom image moving toward them. They all heard the voice over the wind and the waves, the invitation to come and join Him in His stroll across the Sea of Galilee. But everyone stayed in the boat. Everyone except one man. The impetuous one. The one who acted first and thought second. He climbed over the side and started walking toward Jesus.

It wasn't until he had traveled several yards that Peter's mind reminded him of the laws of nature: boats float, people sink, especially during storms. Faced with such logic, he sunk and was forced to cry out for help. No one else had to cry out for help. No one else had to rely on Jesus to deliver them. Everyone else stayed in the boat.

I would like to talk to Peter someday. I want to know what made him think that he could actually walk on water. Maybe it was the same bravado that caused him to pull out his sword and start swinging on the night Jesus was arrested. No one else offered any resistance to the crowd, yet Peter was willing to fight and die if need be for the Savior. His sword fight ended much like his stroll on the Sea of Galilee. Jesus intervened and delivered Peter from the mess he made for himself. The Lord was looking ahead to the day of Pentecost. He knew that He had too much in store for Peter to let him blow it.

That wasn't the last time Peter experienced the Lord's deliverance. After Pentecost, after his impulsiveness gave way to faithfulness, he still found himself in situations far beyond his control. The Lord never forgot Peter. From angry crowds and prison cells, the Lord delivered him time after time after time.

The words Peter penned in the second book of the Bible that bears his name mean much more in light of his history. "The Lord knows how to rescue godly men from trials" (2 Peter 2:9). Peter cited Lot and Noah as examples of God's deliverance, but I wonder if he thought back as he wrote to the middle of the night on the Sea of Galilee or to the day the angel came and let him out of jail. I'm sure he did, for I cannot read these words without thinking back to times God has rescued me. The Lord knows how to rescue godly men. Even if we hesitate to put ourselves in that category, this promise applies to us as we follow Christ by faith.

I'm glad it does. I need it. Day after day I find myself in situations beyond my control. Trials strike and I am rendered helpless. Difficult people make sure my life stays difficult. Other times I make shortsighted decisions and the consequences are more than I can bear. Even when I make the right decision, when I know I am doing God's will, the road He takes me down is not always pleasant. Some harsh surprises lie ahead, surprises I would rather live without. I know I could live without temptation; unfortunately it doesn't seem to be able to live without me. Every day temptation comes by to spend a little time with me. I cannot get rid of temptation's unwelcome company or resist it by sheer willpower alone. My flesh wants to give in and my spirit is losing the argument against it. Like Peter on the waves, I need help.

And the Lord freely gives it. The psalmist wrote: "The salvation of the righteous comes from the Lord; he is their stronghold in time of trouble. The Lord helps them and delivers them; he delivers them from the wicked and saves them, because they take refuge in him" (Psalm 37:39–40).

God delivers everyone who takes refuge in Him. No pit is too deep nor is any trial too dark for Him. Whatever we face—trials, temptations, evil people, even death—He is there to rescue us. The Lord never slumbers; He never forgets about us. He always comes through at just the right moment.

I find the most amazing part of this promise of deliverance is that He rescues us from ourselves. As I look back on my life I see an embarrassing pattern emerging. I cannot take much credit for the direction my life has taken. Long ago, when I wanted God to leave me alone, He refused to do so. Later, after I surrendered to His will, I kept trying to make improvements on all that He had in store. Rather than patiently wait for Him to open the right doors, I would run headlong trying to open them myself. He delivers me from the tyranny of myself in order that I might experience the joy that comes from obeying Him.

Obeying God can be a dangerous thing. Those

who follow Him by faith rarely get to stay in the boats of safety and security. In C. S. Lewis's *Pilgrim's Regress*, the Guide announces: "You all know . . . that security is the mortals' greatest enemy."

The words of the Guide are truer than any of us realize. The security we crave is really our enemy. It prevents us from setting out by faith into the unexplored territory that lies ahead of us as we walk with Christ. God's promise to rescue and deliver us gives us the confidence we need to boldly follow, even if it means climbing out of a safe, dry boat to walk with Him across a stormy sea.

37

DISCIPLINE

"My son, do not make light of the Lord's discipline, and do not lose heart when he rebukes you, because the Lord disciplines those he loves, and he punishes everyone he accepts as a son." Endure hardship as discipline; God is treating you as sons. For what son is not disciplined by his father? (*Hebrews 12:5–7*)

I don't like roughing it. I don't like sleeping on the ground or living off the land. If I had been born a few hundred years ago, I probably would not have survived childhood. Waterbeds and microwave ovens are gifts from heaven, and I don't know what I would do without them. Yes, I am soft, a product of the modern age. My idea of primitive transportation is an old Chevy with a manual transmission and no air-conditioning. I never walked five miles to school in the snow (all uphill). Comfort and convenience are the marks of my generation, and I am glad.

It is hard for those of us who have never lived through real times of deprivation to appreciate the words of Hebrews 12. "Endure hardship as discipline," the writer is exhorting us. Accept hard times and inconvenience as an act of love from God. Rejoice when forced to struggle, when life becomes less agreeable. Don't complain, be glad. Embrace trials and suffering, for God is sending them our way to fulfill a promise. Long ago He told us He would adopt us into His family if we would cling to His Son by faith. Now He shows His sincerity by treating us like members of His family. He is treating us like sons through the promise of discipline.

Every child of God will experience His discipline. God loves each one of us too much to leave any of us out. The writer of Hebrews quotes the third chapter of Proverbs, as he tells us that "the Lord disciplines those he loves, and he punishes everyone he accepts as a son" (Hebrews 12:6; Proverbs 3:12). Everyone. If we are not disciplined, we are not God's children (Hebrews 12:8). The mark of a child of God is the constant presence of God's correction and discipline in his or her life. They are acts of His love, reminders that He is involved in our lives.

The Lord never read any modern books on parenting. No one ever informed Him that the best way to get through to us is by reasoning with us. If we engage in some action that displeases Him, we may think He needs to talk to us about it. After all, we may have a very good reason for doing what we are doing. Talking with us could be illuminating for both God and us. He may come to a better understanding of human nature and realize that we are simply learning to explore our world and the options before us.

God never read any of this advice, however. He operates in the old-fashioned way. Rather than shower us with every good thing in order that we might learn to enjoy life, He works through hardships to mold our character. Before you and I jump to the conclusion that He is narrow-minded and cruel, we need to remember that He is God. He knows what we need.

Discipline is never pleasant to receive, but God

is not capricious in what He deals out to us. Every act is part of His loving plan to transform us in the image of His Son. He wants us to share in His holiness (Hebrews 12:10), and He will do whatever it takes to bestow this privilege upon us.

We will never share in His holiness until we win the struggle against sin. Discipline makes victory possible. Through discipline God turns our failures and our sins into teaching points. He allows the consequences of our actions to fall upon us, even though He forgives the sin itself. By doing so He breaks our love affair with sin. Without sin's consequences we will never learn to hate it as much as God does. There are also times when God's discipline takes the form of outright punishment. Again, He is faithful to forgive. Punishment is a teaching method in the hands of God toward His children, not a form of revenge.

King David learned this lesson the hard way. In the eleventh chapter of Second Samuel we find him committing adultery, lying, and murder, acts we never expected from a man after God's own heart. The Lord moved quickly and decisively against the man He established as king. The child conceived in David's act of passion died shortly after his birth. Amnon, one of David's sons by another wife, raped David's daughter Tamar. In revenge David's son Absolom killed Amnon and later drove David himself from his throne. All of this came upon the king even after he cried out, "Have mercy on me, O God . . . blot out my transgressions" (Psalm 51:1). God heard David's prayer and blotted out his sin. Yet He loved David enough to punish him like any loving father would do.

Not all discipline comes as punishment for our sins. If it did then we could expect to see our lives become more pleasant with fewer hardships as we learned our lesson and stayed away from sin. But discipline is more than a negative action that follows our rebellion. The term translated "discipline" carries the idea of educating and training. Other terms found in the twelfth chapter of Hebrews come from the world of athletics and describe the process of training an athlete. God uses hardships to train us in order that a harvest of righteousness and peace might overflow from our lives (Hebrews 12:11). The rigors of training are long, difficult, and boring. But no world-class athlete ever succeeded without them.

God is working to make us something far greater than Olympic champions. He wants to make us like Himself in every way: holy, righteous people who reflect His character to the world. Such lofty goals can only be achieved through the rigors of training, the hardship of discipline.

38

POWER

"But you will receive power when the Holy Spirit comes on you; and you will be my witnesses in Jerusalem, and in all Judea and Samaria, and to the ends of the earth." (*Acts 1:8*)

Powerless. Anemic. Battered. Ignored. The rolls of American churches burst with millions of names, but we do not know where most of our members are on any given Sunday. We've tried our hand at lobbying Washington. Occasionally a politician or two sits up and takes notice of us. They come and speak at meetings in our towns, where they reaffirm our worth and pledge to fight with us for traditional family values. But nothing ever seems to change in our nation.

We try to stand up and be counted. We try to make our voice heard. We try to be salt and light in our nation, to turn it back to God. But in the end we feel defeated and powerless. The gates of hell seem to be doing a pretty good job of prevailing over the church of the late twentieth century.

Strong. Influential. Impossible to ignore. World-changers. The earliest generations of Christians rocked an entire empire. Cities rallied against them but could not silence them. Emperors unleashed the full fury of the state against them, yet in the end the empire was swallowed by that which it tried to destroy. Only the poor and weak, the outcasts, would dare associate with the early Christian church. But that was enough. From a small band hiding in an upper room to an international force in one generation, the early church epitomized the definition of power. Nothing could stop it. The gates of hell threw its full fury against the church of the first century and could not prevail. Its members were world-changers.

A lot has changed in two thousand years. The first-century church was composed primarily of lower-class, uneducated people. By most standards they were poor, the kind of people the movers and shakers find easy to ignore. Today the church is an imbedded part of middle-class America. Church leaders regularly are granted an audience with those in the seats of power, from the president to the leaders of Congress. The first-century church met under trees and in homes. We enjoy facilities with everything from padded pews and air-conditioning to our own gymnasiums, aerobic centers, and bowling alleys, not to mention state-of-the-art light and sound equipment. Compared to those who first started out with Jesus, the church of today has everything they never had. But we lack the most important thing, the very thing Jesus promised to give us before He departed: power.

"You will receive power when the Holy Spirit comes on you." Jesus' words are simple and straightforward. He guaranteed power to His followers to carry out His mission. Jesus had alluded to what this power would do, "I tell you the truth, anyone who has faith in me will do what I have been doing. He will do even greater things than these" (John 14:12). Throughout the book of Acts we see this power in action. The lame were healed, the dead were raised, and the gospel spread throughout the world. On the day this power was first poured out, three thousand people were saved, and that was only the beginning.

The promise of power for the people of God to fulfill the mission of Christ is as real today as it was two thousand years ago. Massive awakenings do not have to be something we read about in books. God can and will do amazing things in our generation. The church does not have to be on the retreat. The Lord promises to give us the power to advance, to take our world with the gospel. But a few changes must first be made.

The church in America at the close of the twentieth century is very much like the church of Laodicea addressed in Revelation 3. Like the Laodiceans, we say we are rich and do not need a thing, but we are lukewarm at best. We have fallen in love with the world and the things of the world. Materialism and wealth choke us and keep us from being effective for God. Some among us have embraced a theology that exalts perishable goods as the measure of God's blessing, in effect reducing God to nothing more than a means to an end. Like the church in Laodicea, we need to realize how spiritually bankrupt we are and humbly repent before God.

We have also become confused as to the purpose behind the power of God. Somewhere along the line we thought it was meant for changing laws and creating a social atmosphere conducive to family values. We began to seek God in order that He might make this world a better place to live. But

this world is not our home. The power of God that
flows from the Spirit of God comes that we might
take the gospel of Christ to the world. Peter, Paul,
and John never led a protest march against Nero's
social policies. They never organized a boycott
against the city of Corinth. Instead they preached
the good news of Jesus and refused to be silent.
Sadly, I find that the church today is the most vocal
about matters without eternal significance, and
silent when it comes to communicating the radical
call of Christ to the world.

The promise of power is as real today as it was
two thousand years ago. We will only experience it
when we imitate those first hearers and leave everything behind to follow Christ. Their influence had
nothing to do with their size, wealth, or social
standing, but it had everything to do with their
brokenness before God. Our Lord is looking for
humble people, people who have turned their backs
on all the world has to offer, people who have taken
up their cross to follow Christ. These are the ones
upon whom God will pour His Spirit with power.
These are the ones who will change our world.

39

WISDOM

> If any of you lacks wisdom, he should ask God, who gives generously to all without finding fault, and it will be given to him. (James 1:5)

Driving past a church the other day I read this statement on its message board "Life never asks questions faith cannot answer." I kept heading east on Highway 40 while the words danced in my head. *Life never asks questions faith cannot answer.* Maybe I am too cynical, but I find life constantly throws questions at me that my faith cannot answer. Call me unspiritual if you like, but I cannot tell a ten-year-old boy why his father walked out the door, never to return. I cannot tell a grieving wife why her husband died at the young age of forty-eight. I cannot tell a fifty-year-old man why he was laid off his job. I can offer all sorts of spiritual sounding sayings, but I cannot give them the answers they really want to hear. I cannot tell them why their lives have taken a sudden turn for the worse.

No one can.

Of course, God could. Maybe He will someday. But He never says that He will. Of all the things God promises and of all the things He could promise there is one thing He never guarantees: He never promises to give us answers. Never. God did not offer any explanations to Job when his world fell apart. He never explained Himself to Jeremiah when the prophet complained of the prosperity of the wicked. He didn't answer Habakkuk when he asked how the Righteous One could tolerate the evil Babylonians. God does not promise to give us answers.

But He does promise to give us wisdom.

James heard the questions of life ringing in his ears. He watched his oldest brother hang on a cross and die. As the pastor of the church in Jerusalem, he cared for a flock of poor outcasts. Between the contempt of the Jews and the famines that struck Palestine, he led a group of people who must have wondered if life could get any worse. Their pastor never answered the pressing question of why they were suffering or why their lives were so much worse than the Gentile believers in Antioch. In the place of answers James held out a promise, "If any of you lacks wisdom, he should ask God, who gives generously to all without finding fault, and it will be given to him" (James 1:5).

Answers try to help us sort out our situation from a natural viewpoint. They fill in information regarding how and why and how long. The search for answers looks for an explanation, as if knowing that a plane crash was caused by mechanical failure rather than pilot error can lessen the grief we feel. Unfortunately, answers are not always accompanied by understanding. For that we need wisdom.

Wisdom opens our eyes to see life from God's perspective. It is short on explanations, but long on providing understanding. We may never know the hows and whys behind the trials we endure, but wisdom doesn't need either to flourish. Wisdom looks past the questions of life to see God sitting on His throne. It reassures us that He is in complete control. And wisdom—not explanations—will be given, the Scripture declares, when we ask God for it.

James links the need for wisdom with trials. Earlier we explored his command to consider the various trials we face as pure joy. How can we do such a thing? Wisdom shows us the way. Through wisdom we realize that trials are not random acts of a cold universe. Instead they are tools in the hand of God to reshape our character and bring us to maturity. Our minds still wonder if there couldn't be another way to bring about the same result. Couldn't God make us mature by giving us every good thing the world has to offer? Perhaps, but He has not chosen to work that way. Maturity comes through trials; character through suffering. Through wisdom we trust that God knows the best way to make these a reality in our lives.

Wisdom's value stretches across all of life. Solomon encourages us to seek it as intently as we would hidden treasure. Its worth is far greater than perishable things like silver and gold. Wisdom protects us and leads us in the paths of righteousness. A man who tackles life without it is little more than shark bait. No one can last long without wisdom. With it, we can have peace in the midst of any situation, for the Lord will guard our feet and establish our lives. "[Wisdom] will set a garland of grace on your head and present you with a crown of splendor" (Proverbs 4:9).

Something this valuable must be very expensive. Yet the Lord tells us that wisdom is ours for the asking. "If any of you lacks wisdom," James writes, "he should ask God, who gives generously." Solomon tells us in the book of Proverbs that the beginning of wisdom is to fear the Lord (Proverbs 1:7). The two exhortations—ask for wisdom and fear the Lord—go hand in hand. To fear the Lord is to see Him in His glory and splendor, to respect and revere Him, to trust Him. Without the fear of the Lord, no one ever asks for wisdom. They keep on looking for answers and offering suggestions to heaven.

Wisdom humbles us before God and looks to His purpose and plan in everything. When heartache strikes, ask God for wisdom. When we do not understand what God could possibly be up to, when we wonder if He is in control at all, ask God for wisdom. When we are discouraged and ready to quit, ask God for wisdom. And He will freely give it. The questions may still go unanswered, but you will have His assurance that He is still in control, still at work, still God. Wisdom leads us to trust Him.

40

COMFORT

> Praise be to the God and Father of our
> Lord Jesus Christ, the Father of compassion
> and the God of all comfort, who comforts us
> in all our troubles, so that we can comfort
> those in any trouble with the comfort we
> ourselves have received from God. For just
> as the sufferings of Christ flow over into our
> lives, so also through Christ our comfort
> overflows. *(2 Corinthians 1:3–5)*

Throughout the pages of this book we have taken
a very realistic look at the promises God makes
to us in His Word. To be completely honest, I
would have rather ignored some of them. Thinking
about the glories of heaven excites me, contemplat-
ing trials and suffering does not. I would not have
done either of us any favors by trying to gloss over
what I find distasteful. As Paul states in 2 Corinthians 1:5, "The sufferings of Christ flow over into our
lives," and they will continue to flow over us until
Christ brings history to a close. And so the promises
have included persecution and discipline along
with blessing and provision.

It is within that which we would rather avoid
that God's greatest promises come to life. If God
placed an umbrella of safety over us and filled our
lives with the best things the world has to offer, we
would never experience the joy that flows from the
comfort only He can give. Paul calls our Lord "the
God of all comfort, who comforts us in all our troubles." Think about that for a moment. To comfort

us in *all* our troubles dictates that He set up a
twenty-four-hour vigil over our lives. Troubles strike
so frequently, so suddenly and without notice that
He could never leave us alone for a moment if He is
serious about keeping His promise. It is hard to
imagine that God would stoop low enough to stay
in such constant contact with us.

But that is exactly what God does. The first promise we explored together was more than a promise;
it was a name. The name above all names. The name
Jesus. In Jesus, God promises to give us Himself. Now
as we come to the end of our journey we come face-
to-face with another promise that is more than a
promise. It too is a name. A name of the Holy Spirit
of God: the Comforter. Part of God Himself, the
third Person of the Trinity, takes up permanent residence inside every follower of Christ. Jesus Himself
promised that He would not leave us as orphans.
"And I will ask the Father and He will give you another Comforter, in order that He might be with
you forever" (John 14:16, author's translation).

The name *Comforter* literally means one who
comes alongside someone and encourages the indi-
vidual, builds him up, and shares his grief. This is a
major part of the ministry of the Holy Spirit in our
lives. He brings the promise of comfort down to
earth and pours it into our hearts. The Comforter
reminds us that God is aware of our struggles and
grief; He is not far away and uncaring. He draws
near to us through the Holy Spirit, the promised
Comforter. His Spirit carries us through our times
of grief; He encourages us when we would rather
give up. He gives us the strength to go forward after
Christ.

The Comforter's primary tools to accomplish all of the above are the very things we've spent the last thirty-nine chapters exploring. He draws on all the promises of God's Word and makes them come alive when we need them most. In the introduction we came face-to-face with the fact that our lives are completely dependent upon God's promises. The promise of comfort reinforces this truth. The comfort we receive from the Holy Spirit of God comes through the Word of God and the promises that fill it. These promises dry our tears and set our sights on heaven.

God does more than dry our tears. As He comforts us He also issues an invitation. The God of all comfort comforts us in all our troubles in order that "we can comfort those in any trouble with the comfort we ourselves have received from God." The Lord of the universe, the Maker and Sustainer of heaven and earth, invites frail creatures of dust like you and me to be the human instrument through which He keeps His promise to others. Heaven can seem so far away, and the Spirit's invisibility is sometimes mistaken for absence. Therefore, God makes His presence known by taking on human flesh and invading real-life situations. And the flesh He takes on is yours and mine. We comfort others with the comfort we have received from God. Call it an interactive promise. I call it the highest privilege any human being can ever receive.

This is our calling. We are surrounded by hurting people. Some are brothers and sisters in Christ; others haven't a clue as to who God is or what He is like. The God of all comfort constantly moves us out into this mass of hurting people in order that

He might show them how much He loves them through us.

Fear makes us dig in our heels and resist. We don't know what to say or what to do. God's comfort sweeps away our fear. All we need to do is share with others the comfort we have received from God. The Comforter who dwells within us will make sure we know what to say. The most effective thing we can do is imitate God and do for others what He has done for us. He came to us when we needed Him the most and loved us. We must do the same.

As we do, we can finally appreciate the full joy and wonder of this promise, a promise of God Himself.